Halloween
Costumes & Other Treats

Stuart Schneider
& Bruce Zalkin

Schiffer Publishing Ltd

4880 Lower Valley Road, Atglen, PA 19310 USA

Acknowledgments

The authors wish to thank the following people who graciously agreed to let them photograph parts of their collections or contributed photographs or information and without whose help this book would not have been possible: Peter Nason (who spent an incredible amount of time assisting with research and photo captions, and whose insight helped to put the costumes in perspective); Ralph Price, who contributed many non-costume items from his collection; David Bertolino and Spooky World (America's Horror Theme Park in Foxboro, Mass. Visit them on the web at www.spookyworld.com) whose Halloween costume collection and museum is the only one open to the public; The National Costumes Association (1-800-622-1321); Jim Roan at the Museum of American History/Smithsonian Institution; Rubies Costume Company; Collegeville/Imagineering's resident expert Sam Cornish; Gary and Sue Peterson; Stephen Shutts; and a personal thanks to the friends and family who acted as models for the costumes.

Library of Congress Cataloging-in-Publication Data

Schneider, Stuart L.
Halloween costumes & other treats/Stuart Schneider & Bruce Zalkin.
    Halloween costumes & other treats/Stuart Schneider & Bruce Zalkin.
    p. cm.
    ISBN 0-7643-1410-6 (Paperback)
    1. Halloween--Collectibles--Catalogs. 2. Halloween costume--Collectors and collecting--Catalogs. I. Title: Halloween costumes and other treats. II. Zalkin, Bruce. III. Title.
    NK6076.5.S358 2001
    394.2646--dc21   2001001546

Copyright © 2001 by Stuart Schneider & Bruce Zalkin

Designed by "Sue"
Type set in Seagull Hv BT/Korinna BT

ISBN: 0-7643-1410-6
Printed in China
1 2 3 4

Contents

Published by Schiffer Publishing Ltd.
4880 Lower Valley Road
Atglen, PA 19310
Phone: (610) 593-1777; Fax: (610) 593-2002
E-mail: Schifferbk@aol.com
Please visit our web site catalog at www.schifferbooks.com or write for a free catalog.

We are always looking for authors to write books on new and related subjects. If you have an idea for a book, please contact us at the above address.

This book may be purchased from the publisher.
Please include $3.95 for shipping.

In Europe, Schiffer books are distributed by
Bushwood Books
6 Marksbury Ave.
Kew Gardens
Surrey TW9 4JF England
Phone: 44 (0)20-8392-8585; Fax: 44 (0)20-8392-9876
E-mail: Bushwd@aol.com
Free postage in the UK. Europe: Air mail at cost.
Please try your bookstore first.

Introduction

Halloween touches the heart and soul with its images and memories. Little kids think the holiday, with its parties and trick or treating, was created just for them. Before the turn of the 19th into the 20th century, young lovers thought that Halloween, the courting holiday, was created for them. Their future could be predicted during Halloween night and they might discover who they would marry, or if they would never marry. In the roaring 1920s adults treated Halloween as a social holiday that offered an occasion to dress up in strange garb, attend parties and dance the night away. In the 1950s, the children again laid claim to the holiday. For a holiday where the notable images are skeletons, witches, ghosts, lighted Jack O'lanterns and monsters, what is it about Halloween that fascinates us and appeals to all age levels?

Halloween has its origins drawn from Celtic lore more than 4000 years ago. Druid priests dressed in animal skins, leaves, and feathers and welcomed in the dead season after their harvest. Wiccans read natural signs, such as cracks in nuts, for hints about the future. Later, Christian leaders declared the holiday a time to honor the saints. Over time Halloween has matured into an incredible holiday. No longer is it just celebrated on October 31st. It is now a season. Beware, the holiday is taking root throughout the world.

Each year more of the strange symbols of our holiday appear in other countries. France has especially claimed Halloween. Hundreds of Jack O'lanterns have lined the grounds around the Eiffel Tower in Paris. In Belgium and Great Britain windows show witches and black cats and homes are decorated for Halloween parties. European customs officers now look for pumpkin seeds in the luggage of those returning home.

In the United States, the professional haunted house industry has blossomed and now has at least two magazines to share information within the business. In October, they appear across the United States. Some of the larger haunted events scare 7500 people per evening and employ up to 100 actors to shock their patrons. Amateur home and yard haunters are appearing in neighborhoods and drawing hundreds of visitors on evenings leading up to Halloween. In some neighborhoods everyone on the street is involved and the local police come out to direct traffic. Amusement parks such as Busch Gardens and Knott's Berry Farm now feature haunted houses in October. Disney's Haunted Mansion runs to full capacity. Universal Studio's Halloween Horror Nights attract tens of thousands of people looking for a good scare. More amusement parks have plans to expand their Halloween offerings. Halloween has become big business.

Television has slowly caught on that Halloween season deserves special programming. Horror movies are featured on television during the month of October. Popular shows have a Halloween episode—two that did an especially good job were Tim Allen's and Rosanne Barr's shows. Halloween parades are also gaining public support. New York City's Greenwich Village Halloween parade, which was broadcast live for the first time in 2000, now draws over 500,000 people and many of the spectators are dressed as spectacularly as the marchers. Cities and towns across the country sponsor their own parades. There is a movement afoot to have more town-sponsored parties on the night before Halloween to cut down on the Mischief Night youth.

Halloween is a multi-billion dollar and growing business in the United States. Costumes, candy, decorations and haunted attractions do their part. Stores start selling Halloween merchandise in August. Many people begin decorating their homes on October 1 and leave decorations up until Thanksgiving.

Halloween collecting is starting to be recognized as a mainstream collecting field. The incredibly active group of people, who collect Halloween items, now spends more in pursuit of their hobby than the collectors of all other holidays. Many people, after having read the first book on Halloween collecting—*Halloween In America* by Stuart Schneider—began to collect or continued to expand their collections. Unfortunately, the target of their desires has become most elusive. There are more collectors than items to collect. No longer can one just go out with a pocketful of money and buy a nice old Halloween piece.

In the past, Halloween items were not saved from year to year like Christmas items. They were generally used and discarded. This scarcity has driven auction prices up to levels that are still considered incredible by most Halloween collectors and downright insane by non-Halloween collectors. Beginners can still find enough to start a collection, but advanced collectors want the rare and unusual pieces such as German-made candy containers, German-made Jack O'lanterns, graphically exciting die cut paper items, and rare Halloween costumes. Unfortunately, as prices rise, reproductions are starting to appear.

The fun, excitement, and recollection of trick-or-treating continues to inspire today's Halloween lovers. Costumes are one of the things closely associated with Halloween and trick or treating. Memories of their own childhood have motivated collectors to seek the costumes that they wore or saw on Halloween. Along with the Halloween collectors, toy and pop culture collectors have been buying up unusual and interesting costumes showing their favorite toy, television shows, movies, or cartoon characters.

Do you remember the musical groups, The Beatles, The Monkees, Josie & The Pussycats, and Kiss? There were costumes for all four. Those with an interest in space exploration can find many costumes with a space theme. Look for the adventure comics of Flash Gordon and Buck Rogers or the television shows of *Space Cadet, My Favorite Martian*, and *Star Trek,* or movies such as *Star Wars* and *Alien*. If you love the newspaper comic strips, look for costumes showing Archie, The Phantom, Mandrake the Magician, and Li'l Abner. If you are more television-oriented, you might want to look for the Road Runner, Bullwinkle, and Scooby Doo. Disney collectors seek the early Disney costumes for Mickey, Donald, Tinkerbell and the Disney television characters such as Zorro and Davy Crockett. Movie collectors are having a field day finding costumes from their favorite movies.

A Short History of Halloween

Halloween was originally a holiday that developed from the beliefs of the Celts (pronounced "Kelts") and their religious leaders, the Druids, more than 4000 years ago. The Celts were farmers, with simple beliefs—good or bad spirits influenced life, death, the weather and the growth of crops. The Celtic year ended with the harvest and the new year began with the coming of Winter. When calendars were established, the year ran from November 1 to October 31. The year's end was celebrated with harvest feasts and family get-togethers. These were times for fortune telling and matrimonial soothsaying.

The Druids would dress in costumes made of pelts and feathers and Wiccans read the future, sometimes by looking at the embers of a fire or reading the lines in a cracked nut that had been thrown on the fire. Much later, in the 18th & 19th centuries, young ladies would adopt these Celtic rituals and take several nuts and name each after possible husbands. The nuts were thrown on burning coals and if they burned evenly, unevenly or exploded, it would be interpreted as a good match, a bad match or spinster hood.

Halloween's symbols evolved from the Celts' concerns. A Celtic concept was the circularity of life. There was no beginning and no end. "Death" represented not the final end of life, but the barren fields at the end of a growing season. At this time of family reunions, the spirits of "dead" relatives were also welcome and they, too, returned home for the harvest festival. Also, the separation between life & death and past & present, called "the veil", was at its thinnest, allowing the ghosts to cross over and join the living. These activities became annual rituals and our Halloween evolved.

As the Christian religion spread into the areas inhabited by the Celts, many adopted Christianity. Although they embraced the religion, they still kept pagan beliefs and celebrations. The Church tried to stop these festivals and substitute Christian holy days in their place. Samhain (usually pronounced "Saw Wan"), the symbol of winter and the dead season, began to be portrayed as the Devil. Celebrators of Samhain were told that they were honoring the Devil, an idea unacceptable in the Christian faith. The festival was replaced, about 800 AD, by a holiday honoring the saints. November 1st was now "All Hallow's Day" ("hallow" meaning "saint"). The evening before All Hallow's Day was All Hallow's Evening, which in its shortened form became Hallow's Even and eventually Halloween.

Harvest celebrations were usually held outdoors and the fall colors became the colors of Halloween. Cornstalks, scarecrows and pumpkins are part of the harvest and the celebration. The outdoors was home to the elves, goblins, fairies and other spirits that inhabited the woods and fields. These too became Halloween images. Fairies and witches flew about during harvest celebration to welcome the spirits and guide them through the veil.

The witch image is one of the most prominent during Halloween. Witches were an important part of the Celtic society, making potions to cure illness, reading the future, or keeping bad spirits at bay. The word "witch" come from the word, "wica" meaning "wise one". Witchcraft was outlawed by the Roman empire about 100 AD, because of its supposed power over the people. Roman leaders perceived witches to be powerful leaders who might teach ideas that conflicted with Roman ideals. Witches were captured and killed. To avoid persecution, witches became secretive. Their gatherings at Halloween would have looked similar to the images familiar in Halloween decorations. Witches stirring cauldrons, others dancing, others under the influence of some potion, bonfires, and costumes were ever present.

Black Cats go hand-in-hand with witches. The black cat was the witch's "familiar" or special animal that helped to channel the witch's powers. It was said that witches could turn into a black cat so that they could blend into the background and not be noticed. The origin of the superstition that you will have bad luck when a black cat crosses your path is based upon the idea that it was a witch crossing your path.

The origin of the Devil image is interesting. In times when animal sacrifice was acceptable, the animal of choice was a goat. A ceremonial dumping of one's sins would take place with the sins being heaped on a goat. This was the original "Scapegoat". The goat would be blamed for all that was wrong or bad and then killed and burned. Look at any image of the Devil. It has a billygoat face.

Ghosts, too, play a major part in Halloween rituals. Late October was the time of the year when the spirits were welcomed back to their earthly homes. The reason for more ghost sightings at this time of the year is that it is easier to see them as Halloween approaches, and since the veil between past and present, and life and death is at its thinnest, spirits can more easily cross over during Halloween.

A powerful image of Halloween is the carved Jack O'lantern. It is recognized almost worldwide as a Halloween image. Traditionally, in The British Isles and during harvest, decorative lanterns, made out of large turnips or other vegetables, were hung outside the home. The custom of hanging lanterns arose from the practice in Scotland and Ireland of putting lanterns along the roadway to guide friends, neighbors and deceased relatives to the harvest festival. A name given to these vegetable lanterns was "Jack of the Lantern" from a legend about a man named Jack. The story says that when Jack died, his soul could not enter Heaven because he was a miser, nor could it enter Hell because he had played tricks on the Devil. Jack's ghost was forced to wander the countryside carrying a lantern made from a turnip until Judgment day. As immigrants came to this country, the American pumpkin, large and bright orange, was substituted for the carved turnip and it became the Jack O'lantern.

The frightening images of the night were further added to by horror movies of the 1930s such as *Frankenstein, The Mummy, Dracula, The Werewolf of London*, and, later movies like *The Creature From the Black Lagoon* and *Nightmare on Elm Street*. These monsters and vampires have become a part of the Halloween lore.

Candy Containers, Figures, Jack O'lanterns, and Other Decorative Pieces

The earliest candy containers appeared around the turn of the century and were made of painted glass. They can be found in the shape of witches and Jack O'lanterns. The paint has a tendency to wear off the surface of the glass, so those with original paint are highly prized. Most have or had a metal top with a little carrying handle. They were filled with tiny pill-shaped candy.

About 1912, German manufacturers began making containers, figures, and Jack O'lanterns of "composition," also called "compo." Composition resembles plaster of Paris but is actually a bit more complex. Here is an old recipe to make a pound of compo.

"Dissolve a quarter pound of flake carpenter glue in 8 ounces of boiling water. Heat a quarter pound of yellow rosin with one ounce of linseed oil. Combine the rosin and glue mixtures and stir in a half pound of whiting until it is the texture of putty. Hair, shredded cloth or paper can be added as a binder. The mixture will harden in 24 hours."

The putty-like composition was formed in a wooden mold. It created two halves of the figure that were then joined together while still soft. The figure was allowed to dry. Each figure was then hand-painted in Halloween colors. With candy containers, the head or a plug in the bottom was removable and the pill-like candy was contained inside. The same process was used to make Jack O'lanterns.

At the same time that compo pieces were being made, other Halloween decorations were being made of pressed paperboard. This was cardboard that was dampened, pressed into a wood mold, and dried. The two halves were then attached and coated with compo or gesso (which is used to coat painters' canvases to obtain a smooth surface) and painted. Pressed paperboard was popular in the late teens, 1920s and probably as late as 1950s. There was an overlap of the different production methods.

A thick paperboard was used to make embossed and die-cut wall decorations with witches, cats, skeletons and other Halloween images during the 1920s to the 1950s. Many of the earlier pieces marked "Made in Germany" fetch a premium over non-marked items.

Jack O'lanterns can be found that are made of compo and paperboard. The more unusual lanterns are painted to look like the devil, a black cat, or even a dog, monkey, or clown. They had cutouts for the eyes, nose, and mouth which were usually backed with thin colored paper. The same lantern with paper eyes, nose, and mouth will sell for at least twice as much as one missing the paper eyes, etc. Some have added ears, noses, or other features that make them stand out among a group of lanterns. These usually sell for $150 or more with some selling for a thousand dollars.

Following the pressed paperboard lanterns were the pulp pieces. They were made of a material similar to that which egg cartons are made from. They are lighter than pressed paperboard, with the 1940s pieces being slightly heavier than the pieces dating 1950s and later. Originally all lanterns held candles and many should show signs of being used. In the 1950s battery-powered lights replaced the candles as plastic replaced pulp.

Reproductions and Fakes

Now that the prices paid for old Halloween pieces are in the hundreds of dollars, copies of old candy containers and Jack O'lanterns and outright fakes are beginning to appear with more regularity. The collector can learn what is out there by first buying all the Halloween books available and finding out what the old items look like. Second, get a level of expertise that comes with buying and selling, or at least monitoring what is being bought and sold. This can be done on the Internet at a site such as eBay. A search of their Halloween section can return thousands of items, new and old. Third is to expand your search and collecting parameters. Buy what others have overlooked. When the wonderful old German composition candy containers became rare, collectors turned to the plastic pieces from the 1950s and 1960s. When they became rare, they turned to decorative paper items. Fourth is to check out what is new each year and collect the new pieces that have some artistic or original content.

Some of the of suspect pieces that have shown up over the past few years are: 1) a full-bodied Devil, composition horn with paper "tongue" that uncurls when you blow it, about 8.5 inches long; 2) a Devil's head made of composition that stands about 4.5 inches tall by 3.5 inch wide (it looks like it was made to attach to a puppet body) and 3) a group of small 3- to 4-inch tall Jack O'lanterns in mint condition. All pieces are always found in mint condition and have a powder-look (flat) finish. They are nicely made. As the story goes, they came out of buildings in East Germany that were closed up for years. When the Berlin wall came down and the West Germans went looking into what remained in East Germany, someone stumbled upon this cache of unopened Halloween decorations that were probably made in the 1930s or 1940s. German toy dealers somehow got the cache and brought them to the U.S.

The story is not to be believed. The pieces are much newer than 1940s. More likely, the old molds were discovered. More caches of old-looking Jack O'lanterns and pressed paper candy containers are coming out of Germany each year. Most of the people bringing them to shows are not selling them as old, but one or two dealers down the line, you can bet they will be offered as vintage pieces.

There are also a variety of newly made old style pulp Jack O'lanterns that sell in some of the antique newspapers. They tend to have a flat bottom rather than having the original circular indented bottom. They will start to appear as vintage pieces in a few years. Additionally, a store in San Francisco has been selling reproduction Jack O'lanterns that have an old shape but are covered with bright glitter. They will not fool anyone who is familiar with the old style lanterns, but someone will eventually offer them as old stock. Buy them now as collectibles rather than later as antiques.

German squeakers, one with a witch head and one with a devil head, have appeared in the last few years. Each has a paper face on thick board attached to a white bellows-type squeaker that is mounted on a six-inch-long wooden stick. The bellows are a rubber material that is usually bright white and very supple.

They are obviously modern reproductions. They are currently being offered by one dealer, who has been advised of their age, as old German pieces. Buyer beware.

One group of items that is not being faked or reissued are old Halloween costumes. They are relatively inexpensive, so far. New costumes are different from the older ones in styles and materials.

Halloween Gallery
Candy Containers and Figures

CANDY CONTAINER, ca. 1920. Halloween Kid, Composition, German made, 4 inches tall. The bottom has a plug to hold the candy. Ralph Price collection. Value $300-325

CANDY CONTAINER, ca. 1905. Glass Jack O'lantern man with most of his paint missing, made in Germany. Opens at bottom. 4.25 inches tall. Ralph Price collection. Value $450-475

CANDY CONTAINER, ca. 1920. A German-made composition candy container of a boy sitting on a Jack O'lantern. The bottom has a plug to hold the candy inside. 3.5 inches tall. Value $375-400

CANDY CONTAINER, ca. 1920. Witch, Composition, German made, 4.5 inches tall. Remove her head to get the candy. Ralph Price collection. Value $350-400

CANDY CONTAINER, ca. 1920. Jack O'lantern man, Composition, German made, 2.75 inches tall. The head removes to get the candy. Ralph Price collection. Value $300-325

FIGURE, ca. 1920. Goblin man, Composition, German made, 8 inches tall. Ralph Price collection. Value $350-400

NODDER, ca. 1920. Jack O'lantern man, Composition, German made, 5.5 inches tall. Ralph Price collection. Value $350-400

FIGURE, ca. 1920. Jack O'lantern man, Composition, German made, 6 inches tall. Ralph Price collection. Value $225-250

CANDY CONTAINER, ca. 1920. Jack O'lantern man in a military costume, Composition, German made, 4.75 inches tall. Remove the head to get the candy. Ralph Price collection. Value $500-525

FIGURE, ca. 1920. Black Cat, Composition, German made, 5 inches tall. Ralph Price collection. Value $225-275

NODDER, ca. 1920. Jack O'lantern man, Composition, German made, 9 inches tall. Ralph Price collection. Value $350-400

FIGURE, ca. 1925. Jack O'lantern man in a chair, Composition, German made, 4.5 inches tall. Ralph Price collection. Value $275-300

CANDY CONTAINER, ca. 1925. Jack O'lantern man, Composition, German made, 2.75 inches tall. The box below opens to hold the candy. Ralph Price collection. Value $325-350

CANDY CONTAINER, ca. 1920. Witch on a broom, Composition, probably German made, 8 inches tall. Remove the head to get the candy. Ralph Price collection. Value $500-525

CANDY CONTAINER, ca. 1925. Witch and Broom, Composition, German made, 3 inches tall. The box below opens to get the candy. Ralph Price collection. Value $425-475

FIGURE, ca. 1930. Jack O'lantern man in a chair, papier mâché, German made, 4 inches tall. Ralph Price collection. Value $150-175

CELLULOID FIGURE, ca. 1935. A fine little girl in witch's costume, Japanese made, 2 inches tall. Ralph Price collection. Value $250-300

CANDY CONTAINER NODDER, ca. 1935. Black Cat, formed paperboard, German made, 5.5 inches tall. Ralph Price collection. Value $300-350

FIGURE, ca. 1935. A plaster devil's head. What an exceptional and scary image! 8 inches tall. Ralph Price collection. Value $345-375

FIGURES, ca. 1935. A pair of Mexican Day of the Dead figures. These stand about 24 inches tall and are made of composition. The Mexican Day of the Dead celebrates the dearly departed in a festive way with figures of skeletons in everyday events. Bakeries make sweet cakes and breads in the shapes of bones and skulls. Value $125-150 ea.

FIGURE, ca. 1945. Jack O'lantern man & woman, Plaster, German (US Zone) made, 6 inches tall. Ralph Price collection. Value $150-200 the pair

This and following page, top left:
CANDY CONTAINERS, ca. 1950. Die-cut
paper board candy wagons. 3.5 inches tall.
Ralph Price and Schneider collections.
Value $45-75 ea.

PLASTIC CANDY CONTAINERS, ca. 1955. A grouping of hard plastic candy containers. The top shelf has three color variations of Jack O'lanterns. The second shelf has two scarecrows on wheels. The shelf itself is quite nice with a cobweb design at the bottom. From the collection of Gary and Sue Peterson.

WAX CANDY CONTAINERS, ca. 1960. Fanny Farmer chewable wax candy containers and a tin hard candy container from the Johnston's Candies of Milwaukee. From the collection of Gary and Sue Peterson.

Wall Decorations

WALL DECORATION, ca. 1920. A die-cut Jack O'lantern man. Embossed pressed paper made in Germany. 19 inches tall. Ralph Price collection. Value $145-175

WALL DECORATION, ca. 1920. A die-cut cat girl. Embossed pressed paper made in Germany. 15.5 inches tall. Ralph Price collection. Value $135-150

WALL DECORATION, ca. 1920. A die-cut flying witch. Embossed pressed paper made in Germany. 12 inches tall. Ralph Price collection. Value $125-140

WALL DECORATION, ca. 1920. A die-cut flying witch. Embossed pressed paper made in Germany. 10 inches tall. Ralph Price collection. Value $125-140

WALL DECORATION, ca. 1920. A die-cut flying witch. Embossed pressed paper made in Germany. 16 inches tall. Ralph Price collection. Value $135-150

WALL DECORATION, ca. 1920. A die-cut walking witch. Embossed pressed paper made in Germany. 7 inches tall. Ralph Price collection. Value $85-110

WALL DECORATION, ca. 1920. A die-cut devil's face. Embossed pressed paper made in Germany. 5.5 inches tall. Ralph Price collection. Value $85-110

WALL DECORATION, ca. 1920. A die-cut witch's face. Embossed pressed paper made in Germany. 6.5 inches tall. Ralph Price collection. Value $85-110

WALL DECORATION, ca. 1920. A die-cut Jack O'lantern face with hat. Embossed pressed paper probably made in Germany. 6 inches tall. Ralph Price collection. Value $85-110

WALL DECORATION, ca. 1920. A die-cut bat on the moon. Embossed pressed paper, probably made in Germany. 5 inches tall. Ralph Price collection. Value $70-85

WALL DECORATION, ca. 1930. A die-cut Jack O'lantern, "Flapper" head. Embossed pressed paper, probably made in Germany. 11 inches tall. Ralph Price collection. Value $95-125

SILHOUETTES, ca. 1935. A package of four-inch silhouettes made by the Beistle Company. From the collection of Gary and Sue Peterson. Value $30-45

Left:
WALL DECORATION, ca. 1935. A wonderful die-cut pressed paperboard Black Saxophone player, German made, 15.5 inches tall. Ralph Price collection.
Value $200-225

Right:
WALL DECORATION, ca. 1935. A wonderful die-cut pressed paperboard crow, German made, 8 inches tall. Ralph Price collection.
Value $100-135

Jack O'Lanterns

Right:
LANTERN, ca. 1920. A die-cut Jack O'Lantern. Flat paper made by Beistle. 9.5 inches tall. Ralph Price collection.
Value $100-135

LANTERN, ca. 1905. A wonderful early four-sided paper lantern. The material is heavy board that has a punched out design and a gilded and embossed design that is backed with colored tissue. 12 inches tall.
Value $200-225

LANTERN, ca. 1925. A German-made pressed paper Devil's head Jack O'Lantern. 3.5 inches tall.
Value $375-425

Left and below:
LANTERN, ca. 1935. A four-sided lantern. Paper board and translucent paper made in Germany. 6.5 inches tall. Ralph Price collection. Value $95-120

LANTERN, ca. 1925. A German-made pressed paper cat's head Jack O'Lantern. 3.25 inches tall. Value $375-425

LANTERN, ca. 1935. Papier-mâché Jack O'Lantern, possibly made in Germany. 5 inches tall. Ralph Price collection. Value $225-275

LANTERN, ca. 1935. Papier-mâché Jack O'Lantern, possibly made in Germany. 5.25 inches tall. Ralph Price collection. Value $225-250

LANTERN, ca. 1940. Paper pulp Jack O'Lantern, possibly. 3 inches tall. Ralph Price collection. Value $125-160

LANTERN, ca. 1940. Paper pulp Jack O'Lantern, possibly. 5.5 inches tall. Ralph Price collection. Value $135-175

Left and below:
LANTERN, ca. 1955. A very unusual Halloweenie Beanie. Sort of a lantern-on-your-head effect. I can see moms trying to make their kids wear this outdoors. "Honey, it will let any cars see you in advance." "Mom, it will make me look like a dork." 6.5 inches tall and made by Clever Things Inc. of Cincinnati, Ohio. Ralph Price collection. Value $75-85

Miscellaneous

HORN, ca. 1935. Gnome or devil's head horn, Papier-mâché, possibly German made, 5.5 inches tall. Ralph Price collection. Value $250-275

TIN TOY, ca. 1946. Halloween bus, A great windup toy bus that was made in "US Zone Germany", 4 inches long. The images are ghosts, owls, witches, black cats, dragons and people. Ralph Price collection. Value $175-200

Halloween Costumes

Early Halloween Costume Use

In the mid-1800s, in Scotland, youngsters would go out seeking treats in costume. The practice was known as "guising" (as in disguise). The celebration of Halloween was brought to this country by the influx of Scottish and European immigrants during the years after the American Civil War. The acceptance of wearing a costume on Halloween grew popular in America during the 1880s and 1890s. The staid Victorians were so prim and proper that they needed a release from their formal lives (imagine women wearing a corset and bustle or men wearing spats, hard starched collars, and a vest). Dressing in costume to go to a Halloween party was fun and was socially acceptable within the limits set by Victorian standards. The earliest costumes were home made.

After the turn of the last Century, women's' magazines began giving instructions for making costumes. Dennison, an office and party goods paper dealer issued a Halloween "how to" pamphlet called *The Bogie Book*. The book was a guide to using Dennison products to decorate. Their first informal issue of 1912 gave tips for making costumes out of their crepe paper. Dennison began selling paper costumes about 1916. They were meant to be worn once and discarded. Few have survived. Other companies caught the spirit and began to offer pre-made costumes. Sears, Roebuck, and Company offered their first pre-made Halloween costume about 1930. Even at less than $2.00 per commercially-made costume, sales remained soft as they were considered a luxury. Most women knew how to sew and could create a costume. With the return of the soldiers in 1945 and the booming economy, people began to spend money on luxuries. Companies such as Collegeville, Ben Cooper, and Halco began to make and sell thousands of ready-to-wear Halloween costumes. The prime collecting period of these boxed costumes is about 1948 to the mid-1970s. The costumes had exciting graphics and were made of silkscreen-decorated cotton, rayon and vinyl.

Most of the earlier costumes are theme costumes. These include witches, scarecrows, cats, clowns, hobos, and gypsies. Li'l Abner's family can be found from the late 1930s. Mickey Mouse and Popeye costumes can be found from the 1930s and 1940s. Although character costumes appeared in the 1930s, the 1950s were the true beginning of the comic character, television, and personality costumes. You could be Felix The Cat, Superman (the 1950s box for the Superman costume warned that wearing the costume did not enable the wearer to fly), Bullwinkle, Mandrake The Magician, Alfred E. Neuman (the *Mad* magazine figurehead), Li'l Abner, and Daisy Mae.

Disney characters were also popular, especially Mickey Mouse. There is a distinct difference between an early and a late Mickey Mouse costume. Mickey was popular, and costumes were made over a period of years, so you should not have too much difficulty finding a good one in nice condition and at a decent price. Also look for Donald Duck, Snow White, Cinderella, Tinkerbell, etc. Many collectors prefer older Disney pieces from the 1960s and before, although there are some great 1970s and 1980s characters. Disney made television

shows in the 1950s and 1960s, such as Zorro, Robin Hood, and Davy Crockett. These shows inspired costumes. If you like a smaller collection, other television personalities were immortalized in costumes and were only made for a few seasons. Examples are *Lassie, Mork & Mindy, I Dream of Jeannie*, Morticia from *The Addams Family, The Munsters, Mr. Ed, Rin Tin Tin*, the Fonz of *Happy Days*, and the list goes on. Sometimes a costume was made for a minor character in a show without any made for the major characters.

Pirates, skeletons, and witches are pretty common from the 1950s, but homemade witches' outfits with hand-sewn decorations are hard to find.

In the 1950s popular outer space television shows that inspired costumes were *Captain Video and his Video Rangers* (1949-56), *Tom Corbett "Space Cadet"* (1950-55), *Space Patrol* with Commander Buzz Corry (1950-55) and *Rocky Jones "Space Ranger"* (1954-55). Astronaut costumes from the 1960s were generally made for only one season—Sputnik (1957), John Glenn (1962) and First Man on the Moon (1969). Space television characters such as those from *Star Trek* and *Battlestar Gallactica* were made.

You can collect the old, the new, and everything in between. Fairly new on the scene in recent years are store bought "product" costumes such as Tootsie Rolls, Life Savers, Hershey Bars, McDonald's fries, Big Mac, Ronald McDonald and a few more. I expect that we will see many more in the coming years. Are they worth collecting? Definitely! They represent the mood of the public in the mid- to late 1990s.

Pop Culture Halloween Costumes

Collecting Halloween costumes is not only like romping through a history of Halloween in the last half of the 20th century; it's also like chopping an imaginary machete through the jungles of pop culture. In this exciting journey, an amazing array of characters appear—Little Orphan Annie in the 1940s, Winky Dink in the 1950s, the Jolly Green Giant in the 1960s, John Travolta in the 1970s, Pee Wee Herman in the 1980s, and that bizarre 1990s family for Duracell batteries, the Puttermans. One could easily view 20th-century Halloween costumes as being a road map through pop culture history.

Some of the finest costumes come from the 1940s and 1950s. Radio and the funny papers made their own stars, like Little Orphan Annie, but the advent of television in the 1950s opened the door for this new kind of culture to find a permanent nest in seemingly every living room. Pop culture became America's main culture, and Halloween costumes reflect this.

Lucille Ball was the queen of television, and *I Love Lucy* quickly emerged as the Gold Standard of 1950s situation comedies. So it seems inevitable that a costume was modeled after the great redheaded celebrity. Other favorites of the day immortalized for Halloween apparel include Charlie Weaver, Red Skelton and Laurel & Hardy. Sadly, no costume was ever modeled after TV's king, Milton Berle, but then again it could be safe to say that Berle's signature laugh-getter—cross-dressing—was not considered vogue for the general public to emulate in the conservative Fifties.

TV also boosted the cartoon characters of the day, and Halloween costumes represent this, too. The network executives realized early on that children were home from schools on Saturdays, so they programmed Saturday mornings strictly for the kiddies. Hanna-Barbera became a major player at the time with Huckleberry Hound, that blue canine who would unmercifully croon "My Darling Clementine" at the drop of a straw hat. MGM's Tom and Jerry, Disney's Mickey Mouse, Warner Brothers' Tweetie Bird and even little-known cartoon characters like Buzzy the Crow (from Paramount's "Harvey Cartoons") made numerous appearances on Halloween shelves in the 1950s. Puppets like Kukla and Ollie were enshrined in Halloween vestries, but their live-action compatriot, Fran, was not.

As grand as the 1950s were, the 1960s were really the decade where the most memorable pop culture costumes emerged. Morticia Addams, the black-clad matriarch of the Addams Family abode, resembles a death-robed Vampira. Coil Man from *The Impossibles*, the genie Shazzan (a costume that actually lights up), Bird Man, Space Ghost, and Bingo from *The Banana Splits* were all popular October 31st attire. There are costumes modeled after toys—Barbie, GI Joe, Captain Action and even Slinky. TV shows spawned a great number of classic costumes—Barnabas Collins from *Dark Shadows*, a bearded Goliath from *Land of the Giants*, and a dolphin mask for *Flipper*. There's a Soupy Sales costume topped with black peach-fuzz for the children's enjoyment. Or how about the Fab Four? Yes, all four Beatles—John, Paul, George and Ringo—were re-created for trick-or-treating, complete with amazing moptops and matching pinstriped suits. If the Beatles weren't your pop group of choice, then how about the Monkees? Strangely enough, the Monkees costumes came in two varieties—pants for the boys, mini-dresses for the girls. That's right, there's a Micky Dolenz costume that comes with its very own skirt!

The 1960s started out quite quietly. John F. Kennedy was elected President, and Motown just began its soulful reign on the pop charts. A Kennedy costume, as well as one of First Lady Jackie, was released during this time period, Camelot's heyday. But everything abruptly, and tragically, changed with Kennedy's assassination on November 22, 1963. The 1960s—a decade of turbulence and change—would become the most horrifying, most exciting, and perhaps most important decade of the 20th century.

The Vietnam War split the country, and the hippies pushed their peace-love-and-flowers message throughout the streets of America. Interestingly, Halloween costumes depicted this great divide. A Green Beret costume was perfect for the Hawks, while a groovy Hippie costume, with psychedelic glasses and daisies in the hair, was for children who wanted to tune in, turn on, and understand all the lyrics to "White Rabbit." Halloween-induced psychedelia hit its pinnacle with the *Yellow Submarine* Blue Meanie costume—a surrealistic smorgasbord splashed with vibrant colors; it looks like a Peter Max painting sprung to life. And Sid and Marty Krofft's H.R. Pufnstuf, a multicolored dragon that's an obvious relic from the Age of Stoning, makes for what might be the finest costume of all, aesthetically speaking.

Halloween costumes grew increasingly slicker in the 1970s. There are the typical Hanna-Barbera outfits—Josie and the Pussycats, Hong Kong Phooey and Scooby Doo. You'll also find such 1970s notables as the Bionic Woman, Bruce the Shark

from *Jaws*, Mr. Kotter, Chuck Barris from *The Gong Show*, various monkey-faced citizens from *Planet of the Apes*, a *Saturday Night Live* Conehead and even members of the rock band Kiss (with real hair!). The 1980s carried on this tradition of slick character outfits, with E.T., the Smurfs, He-Man, Strawberry Shortcake and the cute equestrians from *My Little Pony* as representatives.

Of course the 1990s had their share of pop culture heroes who in turn were depicted in various Halloween costumes: Bart Simpson, Pikachu, even Power Puff Girls. And as we enter a new millennium, you can feel safe enough to bet the mortgage on your house that this trend toward licensed character costumes will continue to grow bigger than ever.

Costume Companies

Halco (J. Halpern & Co.) of New York was an early company that was an early licenser of character costumes. Some of their early costumes are Mammy and Pappy Yokum, Li'l Abner's parents. Halco costumes very often have a full body image on the costume. The other companies tended to end the design at the waist, but Halco often included the design on the legs. They produced many MGM characters such as Mighty Mouse, Charlie Chan, and Droopy the Dog.

Collegeville, now Collegeville-Imagineering, L.P. (a division of Rubies Costumes), may be one of the earliest makers of boxed costumes. Collegeville began in the small Pennsylvania town of Collegeville as early as 1909. It started out as a flag making company but caught on that Halloween was a seasonal business that should not be ignored. Their flag seamstresses began making costumes in the late 1920s. In the 1930s, they licensed Hopalong Cassidy and the ventriloquist dummy, Mortimer Snerd. In 1937, their main line included Pirates, Chinamen, Patriotic, Drum Majors, Clowns, Dutchmen, Sheep Herders, Gypsies, and other peasant-style costumes. Sometimes their early costume boxes only say "Masquerade Costume" (although this does not definitively mean that it was made by Collegeville). They were located in farm country that did not have many telephones. Their phone number in 1937 was 220, it expanded to 3811 in 1939 and became Huxley 9-3811 in 1961. During most of their existence, they also maintained offices at 200 Fifth Ave, room 434, New York City and in Philadelphia at 716 Chestnut Street. The company bought a makeup and makeup accessories company in 1991 and its name became Collegeville/Imagineering. It was acquired by Rubies Costume Company in 1996.

Collegeville's major competition was Ben Cooper, another maker of boxed costumes. Ben Cooper was located in Brooklyn, New York and is believed to have gotten started in the late 1930s. The company stayed in the Cooper family for most of its existence. Cooper made a range of costumes that differed in price and style. There was an economy line, often containing generic designs, a TV & Personality line featuring current characters on television shows and famous people, a playsuit line, a tiny tot's line, a young adult's line, a monster line, and more recently, specific lines for a single cartoon, such as Strawberry Shortcake, or movie, such as Star Wars. The different costume companies scurried to be first when it came to licensing cartoon characters. Sometimes one company held a character for years. With others, the same character was made by a different costume company a few years after the first company produced the costume. When safety became an issue for trick-or-treaters, Ben Cooper made a Safety First line of costumes. These featured larger eye holes and reflective designs on the costume. The company suffered hard times in the 1990s and their assets were acquired by Rubies Costume Company in 1992.

Bland Charnas' name appears on many fine costumes but almost nothing is known of the company other than their existing costumes. They had offices at 200 Fifth Ave, room 518, New York City. Bland Charnas produced a line of Hanna-Barbera costumes such as Touche Turtle, Wally the Lion, and Lippy the Lion.

Rubies Costume Company is the leading costume company in the world today. They were founded in 1951 by Rubin and Tillie Beige as a small costume shop in Queens, New York. The family still owns the company and it has manufacturing plants across the country and around the World.

Costumes, Play suits and Pajamas

It would seem that a costume is a Halloween costume for all intents and purposes, but that is not the case for this book. The collector may find an old costume that was used in a high school or regional theater play. For the most part, these are not Halloween costumes. They are collectible in their own right, but they should not be called Halloween costumes. Occasionally, an old photograph is found of people in costume and it is claimed to be a group in Halloween costumes. More likely, it is a theater group. To be a Halloween group, you should see Jack O'lanterns or other Halloween images. There are a number of home-made Halloween costumes that are fun to collect when they are of good quality or show the artistic talent of their maker. Just remember that to be considered a Halloween costume, it should have a Halloween theme or be of the sort that would not have been worn as a costume in a play.

Another group of "close to" Halloween costumes are kid's pajamas that are identifiable with a television or movie figure. Kids may have worn them as Halloween costumes, but they were created to be something that could be slept in night after night and are much heavier duty than Halloween costumes. They were definitely made to be washed.

Are play suits Halloween costumes? Yes, they are simply heavier duty Halloween costumes that kids could wear when playing. They were usually washable, which is unusual for standard Halloween costumes. Batman, Davy Crockett, Superman, Soldiers, Ghostbusters and many current Disney characters are good examples. In the book you will see a King Kong playsuit that came out after the 1976 version of the *King Kong* movie. It is hard to believe that a kid would want to be King Kong for an afternoon of playing with his friends, but the box is marked for the costume and it is heavier duty than the standard Halloween costume of the time.

Halloween costumes were made to be worn only a few times and they were not made to be washed. Washing most Halloween cloth costumes can make the colors run or wash off the decoration. Most Halloween costumes of the 1950s and beyond were made of very thin rayon material that did not hold up to too many wearings. Seam splits appear to be common. An incredible number of Halloween costume boxes survived along with the costumes. The boxes are helpful in dating the costumes and identifying their makers.

Dating Costumes
Materials

The commercial boxed costumes made before 1951 were mostly made of cotton or cotton flannel. Those made from 1952 to the late 1960s, were usually made of thin rayon with a silkscreened design. Some early 1950s costumes also used vinyl. This early vinyl was sometimes used for space costumes, since the material was relatively new and somewhat futuristic to the 1950s buying public. There were "Deluxe" models made of a heavier material or with added pieces such as a wig, belt, or bowtie. Some manufacturers added sequins, glitter, or glow-in-the-dark-paints. About 1971, the manufacturers began to make the upper half of the costume from a silkscreened vinyl. The lower section, legs, and occasionally the arms remained rayon. By about 1976, most parts were vinyl. About 1980, manufacturers wanted to produce costumes that could still sell for under $2.00 so they began making simple vinyl smocks with a mask. Although many of these costumes lack the quality found in the earlier costumes, the illustrations may show inspired design, or they may show interesting personalities which are collectible.

Masks made before 1952 were generally of two kinds: 1) made of a starched muslin material that was formed and painted or 2) a cloth bag with a silkscreened design that went over the head and had eye, nose, and mouth holes cut out. The vacuformed plastic masks that we are most familiar with began to appear in the early to mid-1950s. Ben Cooper and Collegeville also sold masks without the costume. It is interesting to note that even after costume production went overseas to Taiwan and China in the 1970s, the vacuformed masks were generally still made in the United States up to the 1990s.

Here are some popular subjects over the years that can be easily dated:
- 1910s: Cats, witches, ghosts
- 1920s: Flappers, Swashbucklers, athletes such as football and baseball players.
- 1930s: Cats, witches, a few personalities, and clowns
- 1940s: Mickey Mouse, Felix the Cat and a few others, Pirates, Clowns
- 1950s: Pirates, Gypsies, Witches, Hoboes, Superman, Spacemen, Disney characters
- 1960s: People in the news and television shows
- 1970s: Movies and television shows
- 1980s: Movies
- 1990s: Products and Movies

Costume Condition and Care

Costumes are great display pieces. Condition counts, so try to avoid costumes showing fading, stains and running colors unless the costume is really hard to find. Most costumes should not be washed, especially those containing glitter. Colors are often not water resistant. Red is probably the least water resistant. A gentle soak in a bathtub with cool enzyme active cleaner may remove some of the stains without affecting the color, but be sure to test the colorfastness of the material. I find that all rayon or cotton costumes can use a good ironing or steaming. Keep your iron on a low setting and stay away from any plastic parts. You may want to iron from the inside out to protect the silkscreened parts. Often the silkscreen paint is rubber-based. Ideally you are looking for the piece that was worn once or twice and then put back into its box for storage.

Note that the fire-resistant material that was applied to many costumes in the 1950s and 1960s had a tendency to darken and cause brown streaks on the costume. Some discoloration is acceptable on rarer items. Shown in this book is an incredible 1950s Beatnik costume that has stains. It is so unusual, with super beatnik images, and rare that it had to be in the collection regardless of its less-than-perfect condition. Ironing helped a lot. Some of the early material from the 1950s hardens and cracks where the rubberized silkscreen design was applied. There is not much that you can do except to treat them gently. If you were really energetic, you could apply an iron-on liner to the inside of the deteriorating costumes. Since these costumes were not made for archival use, adding iron-on material could end up doing more damage to the costume 50 years from now, so only repair what needs to be repaired. Split seams can be re-sewn.

Boxes are nice to have, add value to the costume, and protect the costume to a certain extent. Since the box is a paper product it will break down with age the same way that an old newspaper turns yellow and becomes brittle. One of the breakdown products created in paper is sulfuric acid. This is what weakens the paper and it can migrate to the costumes, staining them or burning them. An inert material such as mylar film may make a good liner for the boxes. You must store them in a dry area. Moisture is the enemy of costumes.

At a recent antiques show, I found a rare Monkees costume in the box. I opened the box to examine the costume and found a soft ball of shredded material. As I lifted the shredded costume out of the box, three mice jumped out and scurried away. It certainly made me jump and reminded me that mice and costumes do not mix well. Storing your costumes in a barn might not be such a good idea.

Where to Find Them

If you surf the web or have a friend who has access, you must try eBay (www.ebay.com) and search "Halloween Costume" to see what is available and get an idea of where prices are headed. It is also a source for other Halloween items. Toy dealers seem to have the lion's share of old costumes, so a toy show might be a good source. Advertisements in your local newspaper should produce results.

Valuing Costumes

Valuing Halloween costumes is difficult in this quickly changing field. We use a "Supply and Demand" valuation, or what would a willing buyer and a willing seller agree to as a value? An examination of the components of value are helpful. An older item is usually rare, but a rare item is not always older. A 1930s Jailbird costume is probably as difficult to find as a 1966 Captain Action costume, but Captain Action has sold on eBay for $2,025.00 while the Jailbird would probably sell for less than $225.00. Age is not the main determinant of value.

Look at the example of a collector who is attempting to find a certain item for his collection. He values that item many times higher than another person who already has one. That collector might be willing to pay $300 for one piece, but would he buy a second or a third at the same price? It depends upon who is buying, the availability and how badly he wants the item. Also, are you buying from a dealer who makes his living selling collectibles or from a local person who has answered your newspaper advertisement.

Things to Consider

Condition. Condition is an important criteria. An item in mint condition may be worth several times more than one in very fine condition. Damage to a visible part may be a major problem. An item with a piece missing may be worth 25% of one with the piece present. Repair is often possible, but to replace, for example, a costume mask, one needs another of the same costume with that piece. Ask yourself if the price is still a bargain when you have to locate and cannibalize another item for parts. The items in this book are priced in excellent condition although the actual piece shown may vary from good to mint in the box.

Availability, or "Will I ever find another?" Some items are easier to find. Ask yourself if it is just a matter of dollars to acquire an example or is this a once-in-a-lifetime chance to find that item? With a once in a lifetime item, condition should not be the major determining factor. Many items were ephemeral or short lived. All that is left may just be a relic or remembrance of the whole item. On those items, you may never get another chance to buy one and the person behind you may be waiting for you to put it down so that he or she can buy it.

Demand. What does it mean to you? To those growing up in the period covered by this book, some items bring back a flood of memories. To some people, seeing an item is enough. To others, possessing it is required, regardless of the price. There are collectors aplenty in the field of Halloween collecting, and the asking price reflects this enormous demand.

Buy the Best. In comparing Halloween collectibles to other collecting fields, it is expected that prices on Halloween items will continue to rise. Higher prices may be a blessing in disguise. Some people have no incentive to sell a piece for only a few dollars, but if they can get "a lot of money" they will sell a piece. You will pay more but you will get a piece that you may never have another chance to own. Collections can be put together for very little money, but, as has been proven true in every field of antique collecting, the best pieces in the best condition have held or increased in value at a greater rate than the more common pieces. Buy the best that you can afford. Remember, you will rarely regret having paid too much for an item, but you will always regret the good pieces that got away.

Cost. A Halloween costume collection need not cost a great deal of money. Some people collect new items. Using your imagination, a nice collection can be put together within your budget. Exhibiting your collection at a local library can generate new leads to the type of material that you collect.

Investment. We discourage people from "investing" in collectibles. Collecting should be for fun and not just profit. Profits will be come if you collect the items that you enjoy and at some later time decide to sell. Buying for investment only, means never playing with your things. They could get broken. Buying, selling, and trading items can help you hone a collection to those items that bring you the most pleasure.

The Illustrations and How They are Arranged

The illustrations of the costumes are arranged by category, and then alphabetically within that category and chronologically within the costume name. For example, under Cartoons, Comics and Animated Characters you will find Atom Ant, followed by Bailey's Comets and others, then to Bullwinkle (early examples), Bullwinkle (later examples) and so on. The outer space costumes are compiled differently and are arranged chronologically to show the transition from fantasy to reality.

Some costumes presented a challenge as to where they should be located. Should Bozo the Clown be under Television Shows, Clowns, or Personalities? You will find him under Clowns. Should the Smurfs be located under Toys and Games or under Cartoons? They are located under Cartoons since the costumes were made about the time of the television show and not at the time of the toys. Star Trek had costumes for the television show

and for the movie. Some are under Television Shows and others under Movies. Some characters are under their own name while others are under their show name. This book contains an index and you should expand your search by checking the index after you look in the category that you feel is correct.

We have included a value guide to help collectors. It is often said that a price guide is out-of-date the moment that it is published. Do not let that affect your use of a value guide. A value guide is comparative. It allows you to compare two items to determine if they are of comparable value. It is useful in buying and trading and it can help give you a feel for the rarity of a piece.

Remember, two is a coincidence, three is a collection. Happy hunting!

Costumes

HALLOWEEN PARTY, ca. 1935. A group of costumed kids at a Halloween party. There are clowns, witches and one kid whose mom hadn't a clue.

COSTUME AD, ca. 1954. A wonderful Woolworth's Advertisement showing three costumes and four masks that they were selling in 1954, plus the hard plastic candy containers available.

ADVERTISING, ca. 1957. A four-foot long poster advertising raisins for Halloween treats. The image is wonderful and shows lots of kids in costume trick-or-treating. Value $200-250

ADVERTISING, ca. 1960. The original artwork for a sign or magazine ad for Collegeville costumes featuring Bugs Bunny and Popeye.

Right & below:
CATALOG, 1961. Pages from the Collegeville catalog showing the Little Lulu, Alfred E. Neuman, Phantom, and Sea Hag costumes, along with a page of rare Mask-A-Rama costumes that featured a giant mask that made up the upper half of the costume.

Shown below and on following page:
CATALOG, 1963. Pages from the Ben Cooper catalog showing the Kennedys, the Flintstones, the Jetsons, Bullwinkle and others.

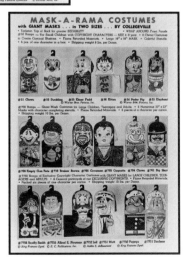

ADVERTISING, ca. 1964. A UNICEF poster shows kids in costume trick-or-treating and collecting for UNICEF. 24 inches tall. Value $125-150

Standard Halloween Themes

COSTUME, ca. 1930. This homemade costume is simple, but there is no mistaking that it was made for Halloween. Sewn cotton material. Value $75-85

DRESS, ca. 1940. This appears to be a well-made, home-made dress with a Halloween Jack O'lantern design. Value $100-125

DEVIL, ca. 1950. Ben Cooper. A rayon Devil costume with a starched cloth mask. This was a frightening costume that would probably not be made today. Value $80-100

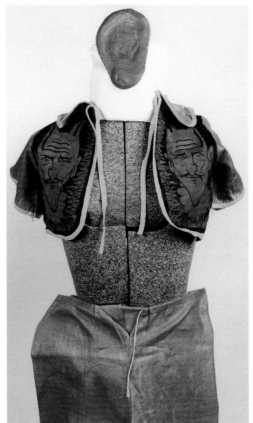

DEVIL, ca. 1950. A starched two-piece cotton Devil costume missing its starched cloth mask. Value $45-50

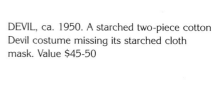

DEVIL, ca. 1952. Ben Cooper. A rayon Devil costume with a starched cloth mask. Value $65-70

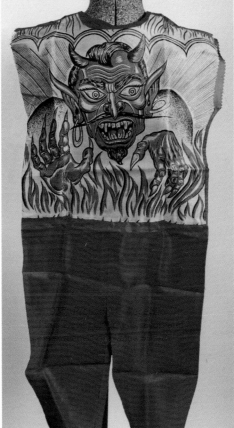

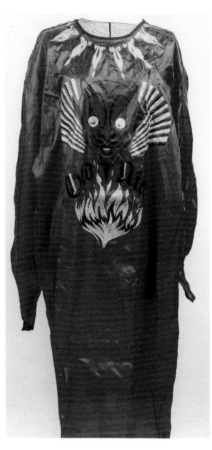

DEVIL, ca. 1952. Collegeville. A rayon Devil "Old Nick" costume which would have had a starched cloth mask. Value $65-70

DEVIL, ca. 1955. Probably Collegeville. The material of this Devil costume is rayon and the design is screened on. Value $75-85

Left:
DEVIL, ca. 1959. Probably Halco. An all rayon Devil's costume with a particularly scary face. Value $35-45

Right:
GYPSY, ca. 1968. The gypsy is an excellent Halloween image because she looks into the future and tells fortunes. Before the 1950s most folks made their own gypsy costumes with shawls, scarves, and beads. After the 1960s, gypsy costumes fell out of favor and were replaced by television character costumes. Value $30-35

DEVIL, ca. 1958. Probably Ben Cooper. This Devil costume has a frightening image, but not as scary as the image that appears in the earlier examples. The material is rayon and the design is screened on. Value $50-55

GYPSY, ca. 1973. Ben Cooper. A Gypsy vinyl two-piece costume. Value $25-30

GYPSY, ca. 1974. A vinyl two-piece costume. Maker unknown. Value $25-30

Left:
MONSTER, ca. 1956. A two-piece rayon Swamp Monster costume missing its mask. Value $65-70

JACK O'LANTERN, ca. 1949. Collegeville. This Jack O'Lantern costume is cotton and comes with a separate hood mask. Value $95-125

MONSTER, ca. 1960. Collegeville. A rayon Monster costume with a plastic mask. Value $45-50

MONSTER, ca. 1963. Ben Cooper. "Monstro, The Monster" was a rayon "Glitter Glo." Value $40-45

MONSTER, ca. 1963. A Monster rayon costume sold at the Grants Stores. Value $25-30

MONSTER MAN, ca. 1964. Halco. Sammy wears an all-rayon costume with a great facsimile of Frankenstein that does not infringe on Frankenstein's trademarks and copyrights. Value $55-65

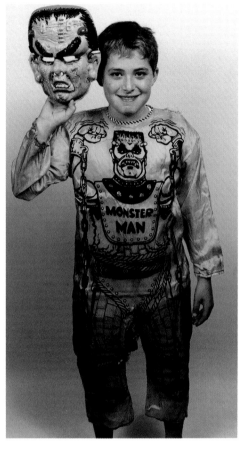

MONSTER, ca. 1968. Also known as The Brute. Value $20-25

MONSTER, ca. 1968. Also known as The Body Snatcher. Value $30-35

Right:
SCARECROW, ca. 1959. Collegeville. One of the enduring images of Halloween, the Scarecrow protects the farmer's crops from thieving birds and has come alive in many horror movies (as well as "The Wizard of Oz"). This is a great costume with the words "Harvest Harvey" written on it. The close-up shows the glitter-finished design. Value $70-80

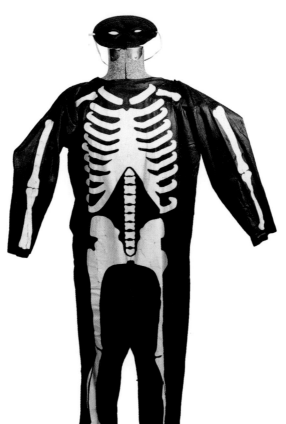

SKELETON, ca. 1950. How do you tell the age of a Skeleton costume? The earlier costumes were made of a thin cotton material. When rayon was developed during the 1940s, it became the material of choice for costumes from about 1950 to the most modern costumes that use a stretchy material. The costume is finished cotton and the design is screened on. Value $25-35

SCARECROW, ca. 1963. Ben Cooper. This particular costume is known as "The Straw Man." Value $45-50

SKELETON, ca. 1952. Ben Cooper. A rayon costume with its starched cloth mask. Value $35-45

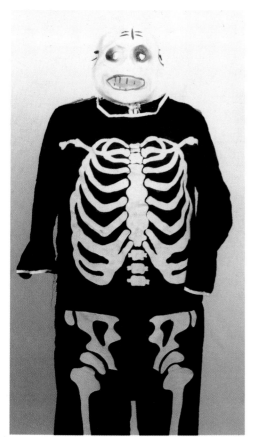

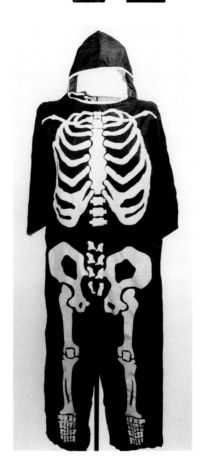

SKELETON, ca. 1952. Ben Cooper. Most of the skeleton costumes are pretty much the same regardless of when they were made. The better skeletons have more unusual designs on the body of the costume. Value $25-35

SKELETON, ca. 1954. Probably Collegeville. Certainly this is an atypical Skeleton costume. The material is rayon and the design is screened on. Value $75-85

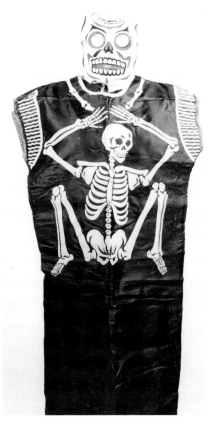

SKELETON, ca. 1974. Bland Charnas. A rayon and vinyl costume, this skeleton has a great personality and nice Halloween theme. Value $40-45

SKELETON, ca. 1960. Collegeville. An unusual Skeleton rayon costume with "Velvet Touch" decorations. Value $35-40

VAMPIRE, ca. 1963. Collegeville. A Vampire rayon costume, she resembles Morticia Addams. The mask has added hair. Value $55-60

Left:
VAMPIRE, ca. 1963. This vampire lady was made to resemble the Morticia Addams costume. The costume has a screened design on rayon. Value $40-45

VAMPIRE, ca. 1974. Bland Charnas. A vinyl Vampire costume. Value $45-50

WITCH, ca. 1940. Probably Collegeville. A witch's costume with a hooded cape, starched muslin mask and skirt. The material is a finished cotton. Value $95-125

WITCH, ca. 1938. Probably Collegeville. A witch's costume with a hooded cape, and skirt. The material is a finished cotton. Value $125-150

WITCH, ca. 1940. Probably Collegeville. A witch's costume with a cape, hat and skirt. The material is a finished cotton. Value $95-125

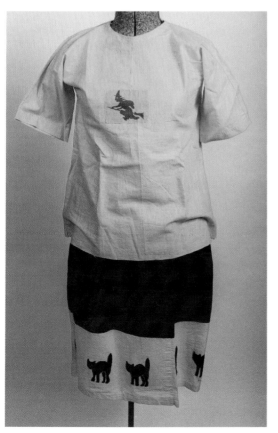

Left:
WITCH, ca. 1940. A witch's costume with a blouse and skirt. This is possibly a Collegeville product, but it could be a home-made costume. Value $75-85

Right:
WITCH, ca. 1945. Probably Collegeville. A witch's costume with a cape and skirt. The material is a finished cotton. The imagery is wonderful, but the material has started to crack and fall off where the screened design has been applied heavily (upper right in the photo). Value $125-150

WITCH, ca. 1951. Probably Collegeville. Also known as Ghastly Gertie. The material is a finished cotton and the design is screened on. Value $95-125

WITCH, ca. 1952. Collegeville. An early vinyl Witch costume with a starched cloth mask. Value $55-65

WITCH, ca. 1960. Collegeville. A rayon two-piece Witch costume and a plastic mask. Value $45-50

Left:
WITCH, ca. 1965. Halco. This rayon two-piece costume continues the tradition of "someone wants to be a witch for Halloween". The graphics are simple but the costume "works" as a witch. Value $35-45

Right:
WITCH, ca. 1976. Ben Cooper. A vinyl witch costume. Value $20-25

BUNNY, ca. 1967. Ben Cooper "Glitter Glo' Costume". The head piece has ears that stand up. Value $40-45

Left:
CAT, ca. 1922. A very rare Dennisons crepe paper black cat costume. These were made to wear once and throw away. The tail came with a crepe tie belt. Value $55-65

CAT, ca. 1940. This simple cat on a fence was made for Halloween. The design is screened onto a cotton material. Value $50-65

Far left:
CAT, ca. 1954. Collegeville. A nice early Black Cat rayon costume with a hooded cloth mask. This costume had a tail. Value $55-65

Left:
CAT, ca. 1954. Collegeville. A Black Cat rayon costume with a hooded cloth mask. This came with a tail. Value $55-65

GORILLA, ca. 1963. Ben Cooper. A rayon Kongo costume. Kongo was apparently a takeoff on King Kong. Value $40-45

GORILLA, ca. 1969. Also known as "Hairy Gorilla." The selling feature of this rayon costume was the "Reflecta-Lites," light reflective stripes on the sleeves that made the costumed child less likely to get hit by a car. Value $35-45

CAT, ca. 1958. Collegeville. Catherine wears a rayon Cat costume with a plastic mask. Value $45-50

CAT, ca. 1965. Bland Charnas. Also called "Scaredy Cat." Screened design on rayon. Value $20-25

Right:
LEOPARD, ca. 1968. Collegeville. A Safari "Leopard" rayon costume. Value $25-30

LION, ca. 1959. Collegeville. John Joe wears a cotton flannel Lion costume with a plastic mask with attached hair. Value $45-55

OCTOPUS, ca. 1963. Ben Cooper. A rare rayon Grippo the Octopus costume. Value $70-75

PARROT, ca. 1953. Collegeville. Classic parrot costume with a separate hood and starched muslin mask. The costume material is a finished cotton. Value $75-95

Left:
MONKEY, ca. 1958. Collegeville. An Organ Grinder's Monkey rayon costume with a tail. Value $45-50

Right:
TIGER, ca. 1968. Ben Cooper. Made of rayon. Value $25-30

Beatniks & Hippies

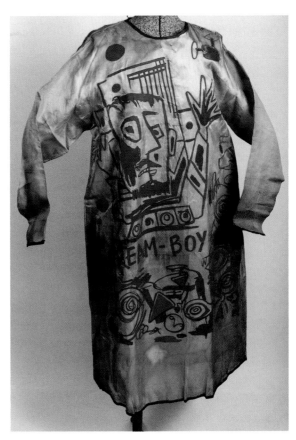

BEATNIK, ca. 1952. Probably Collegeville. The beats were as much a part of pop culture as their groovy spawns, the hippies. But the beats came first, and this costume captures the era exemplified by Maynard G. Krebs, Jack Kerouac and Allen Ginsberg's "Howl." The material looks like rayon and is very thin and fragile. Since this is a long dress-like design, it could have been made for a woman or an androgynous bohemian. Value $125-150

Below:
FLOWER CHILD ca. 1968. Halco. The hippies of Haight-Ashbury were called Flower Children, and this theme ran through various songs of the decade—from "San Francisco (Be Sure to Wear Flowers in Your Hair)" to the "I love the Flower Girl" chorus of the Cowsills' "The Rain, The Park and Other Things." Here is an odd Halloween costume—a literal flower child with flowers for eyes! Value $45-55

HEP CAT, ca. 1948. Collegeville. A costume with hood, tail, and mask. The image is two hep cats dancing to some jive music. It has a bohemian or beatnik flavor. Value $125-175

Right:
BEATNIK, ca. 1963. Ben Cooper. Also known as Birdie Beatnik. The image of the beatnik has left its indelible mark on pop culture—a bohemian who sits in coffee shops sipping espresso, playing the bongo drums and reciting poetry. There was a boy's matching costume called "Buddie Beatnik". TV's most famous beat could be found on "The Many Loves of Dobie Gillis"— Maynard G. Krebs (played by Bob Denver, who later became Gilligan of "Gilligan's Island"). Value $85-95

Right:
HIPPIE; 1960s. Halco. A variation of the hippie garb, which just goes to show what a phenomenon the hippie movement had become. When suburban kids went trick-or-treating as some Jerry Rubin look-a-like, you know the peace-and-flowers movement had really made it. Value $65-85

Far right:
HIPPIE, ca. 1968. Halco. The hippies, also known as Flower Children, exploded in the mid-1960s, and San Francisco's Haight-Ashbury was their capitol. For the cool kids who were into Iron Butterfly and the Electric Prunes, there was this hippie costume. So put some flowers in your hair, crank up some Moby Grape and...trick or treat! Value $65-85

Below:
SPACE PATROL, ca. 1952. Collegeville. "Space Patrol" with Commander Buzz Corey was an early space-themed television series that ran from 1951 to 1955. Buzz Corey was played by Ed Kemmer, and Lyn Osborn portrayed his goofy sidekick, Cadet Happy. Basically, it was a "save the world of the 30th century from space villains" kind of show. All heavy rayon costume. Value $100-125

Outer Space & Robots

Left and below:
SPACE COMMANDO, ca. 1952. Ben Cooper. A wonderful costume with a starched cloth mask. Metalized vinyl and rayon. Value $70-85

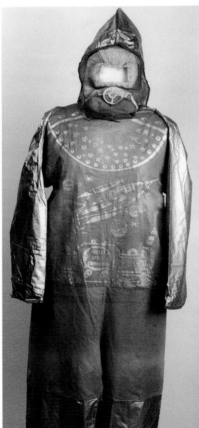

Left:
SPACE MAN, ca. 1952. Collegeville. A rare costume in rayon. It has a starched cloth mask and a silkscreened design of a rocket in space. Value $125-150

Right:
PLANET PATROL, ca. 1952. Halco. A rare costume with four pieces—jacket, hood, belt (not shown) and pants—with a starched cloth mask and a screened design of a rocket in space. Value $125-150

Right:
SPACE GIRL, ca. 1954. Halco. A wonderful Space Girl rayon and early vinyl costume. It had a starched cloth mask. Value $100-120

Far right:
JET MAN, ca. 1954. Ben Cooper. A rare costume in rayon, Jet Man has a hood, mask, red cape and jumpsuit. This was inspired by the early 1950s television space adventure shows. Value $125-150

SPACE ROCKET COMMANDER, ca. 1955. The space race was just about to start. Television shows such as "Captain Video" (1949-1956), "Tom Corbett, Space Cadet" (1950-1955), "Space Patrol" (1950-1955) and "Space Ranger" (1954-1955) awed young boomers. This particular "Space Rocket Commander" costume certainly captures that Fifties sci-fi spirit. Value without mask or box $60-75

MOON MAN, ca. 1956. A great cotton costume missing its mask. Value $75-80

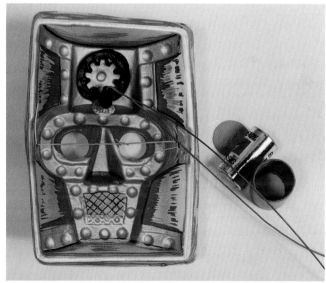

Left and above:
ROBOT, ca. 1957. Ben Cooper. Robots were the technological promise to save mankind in the future. This costume came with a "Flick & Trick Lite-Up Mask"—a mask that had a light bulb above the eyes and wires that ran to a cardboard tube battery holder. Screened design on rayon. A very tough costume to find. Value $125-150

SPACEMAN, ca. 1958. Collegeville. Also known as Satellite Joe. In 1957, the Soviet Union launched Sputnik, the satellite that started the space race. Manufacturers struggled to come out with space-themed products, such as this one. Value $100-120

ASTRONAUT, ca. 1962. Halco (J. Halpern & Co.). U.S. Astronaut costume and mask. In 1961, Alan Shepard became the first American in space. Several costumes were made to commemorate this event. This costume is a screened design on rayon. Value $85-95

CAPTAIN SATELLITE, ca. 1958. Ben Cooper. Dana wears a Capt. Satellite costume. In 1957 the Soviet Union launched the Sputnik satellite. The United States populace was shocked since they believed that the Soviets were a country of peasants. That was the starting gun in the race into space. In 1958 we launched our own satellite aboard a Vanguard Rocket. This screened design on a rayon Halloween costume commemorates that period of time. This one was found without the mask or box. Value $50-55

Left:
SPACE EXPLORER, ca. 1962. Ben Cooper. A rayon Flik & Trik costume. The mask has a light bulb built into the visor. The bulb runs down to a single "D" cell in a holder. Value $50-60

Right:
ASTRONAUT, ca. 1963. Ben Cooper. U.S. Astronaut costume and mask. In 1962, John Glenn became an American hero by orbiting the Earth in a space capsule. Several costumes were made to commemorate the event. This costume is a screened design on rayon. Value $65-75

Left:
MOON MAN, ca. 1963. Ben Cooper. "Moon Man" was a rayon "Glitter Glo' Costume". Two years after the creation of this costume, Neil Armstrong would prove once and for all that aliens do not reside on the moon. But in 1967, such a question was still up in the air: Would the first man on the moon ultimately meet the Moon Man?
Value $60-75

ASTRONAUT, ca. 1965. Ben wears a simple cotton Astronaut play suit. Value $35-45

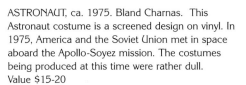

ASTRONAUT, ca. 1975. Bland Charnas. This Astronaut costume is a screened design on vinyl. In 1975, America and the Soviet Union met in space aboard the Apollo-Soyez mission. The costumes being produced at this time were rather dull.
Value $15-20

ROBOT, ca. 1968. Ben Cooper. An all rayon "Chattermouth" costume. On Chattermouth costumes, the mouth would move whenever the trick-or-treater spoke.
Value $75-85

ASTRONAUT, ca. 1969. Collegeville. "White For Night" Man on the Moon costume and mask. In 1969, Neil Armstrong became the first person to walk on the moon. This costume was made to commemorate the event. The costume is a screened design on rayon and was only made for one year. The discoloration is due to the fireproofing material that was applied to the costume.
Value $100-115

Products & Advertising

Left:
BOO BERRY, 1970s. General Mills; Collegeville. There were five monster cereals in all: Count Chocula, Frankenberry, Yummy Mummy, Fruit Brute and of course Boo Berry. Boo Berry was the weirdest of the lot, a cereal that could turn your milk deep blue. The Halloween costume was only available as a premium and not sold in stores. Very rare.
Value $375-425.

Bottom left:
COUNT CHOCULA, 1970s. General Mills; Collegeville. One of the all-time great costumes, children who wore it didn't go trick-or-treating as their favorite cereal vampire. No, they went as an actual box of Count Chocula! This was a mail-away and unavailable in stores. Exceedingly rare, especially mint.
Value $375-425.

ASTRONAUT, ca. 1980. A strange costume with an Astronaut on the moon theme. The material is a man-made non-woven fiber that sometimes appears on the back of vinyl costumes. It is most likely foreign made.
Value $15-20

Bottom center and right:
DURACELL PUTTERMANS, ca. 1996. This costume (or "disguise kit") was inspired by the Duracell television commercials starring the Putterman family. The clan—father, mother, daughter, son—were usually visited by a relative that ran on ordinary batteries and soon ran down; the Puttermans, however, never puttered out since they were powered by Duracell. Separate costumes of Mr. and Mrs. Putterman were created, consisting of a rubber head mask and a vest with a Duracell battery back. The costumes, available only in Canada, are actively sought by flashlight collectors in addition to Halloween costume collectors. Value $30-40 ea.

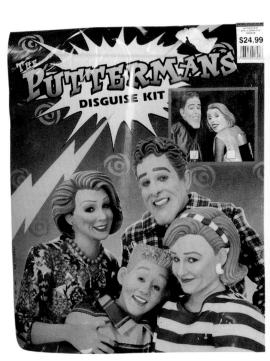

40

ESSO TIGER, ca. 1968. Halco. A very hard to find Esso "Humble Tiger" in rayon by Halco. This costume was created as part of the gasoline company's "Put a Tiger in your tank" advertising campaign. Value $85-95

FRANKENBERRY, 1970s. General Mills; Collegeville. One of the great monster cereals of the 1970s, Frankenberry, whose spokesman was a strawberry-red Frankenstein, actually turned your milk pink as you ate it. This costume was a mail-away and not available in stores. Value $375-425

Left:
HERSHEY KISS, ca. 1985. Hershey's Food Corp.; Collegeville. Odd Halloween wear comes and goes—but maybe none is odder than this "scratch n' sniff" outfit from the middle 1980s. The scratch and sniff spot could be found on the shoulder so the little trick or treater could smell just like chocolate. Value $45-65

Right:
JOLLY GREEN GIANT, ca. 1964. Kusan. Bianca wears a rather rare Costume. This vegetarian spokesperson for Green Giant vegetables (an advertising icon since 1925) is sort of what you get when you mix Goliath with a broccoli spear. He also makes for one fantastic costume. The detail on the mask is exquisite—not just the leafy hair but the dimpled chin too! Value $75-95

KELLOGS' SNAP, ca. 1995. Rubies. Snap appeared in Rice Krispies' commercials. Value $25-30

LIFESAVERS, ca. 1996. Rubies Costume Company. Created in the shape of a pack of Lifesavers using a shiny rayon material, this costume had a semi-rigid foam top to support the shape. It cost $29.95 when new. Value $25-35

McDONALD'S FRENCH FRIES, ca. 1992. This rayon-covered foam-filled item slipped over your head (note the chrome top of the mannequin) and your arms would stick out the sides. Value $20-25

MR. CLEAN, ca. 1968. "Mr. Clean, Mr. Clean, Mr. Clean..." Few commercials could get stuck in your head the way the ads for the all-purpose cleaning product, Mr. Clean, would. This "Mr. Clean" mask is all that is left of the Mr. Clean costume. Value $45-55

Left:
REESE'S PEANUT BUTTER CUP, 1985. Hershey; Collegeville. "Hey, you got your chocolate in my peanut butter!" Here's another odd candy costume, compliments of Hershey. This is a scratch-n-sniff costume, where neighborhood chocoholics could go door to door dressed as their favorite chocolate treat. Value $35-45

Right:
TOOTSIE ROLL, ca. 1996. Rubies. The 1990s were the big decade for product costumes. Value $20-25

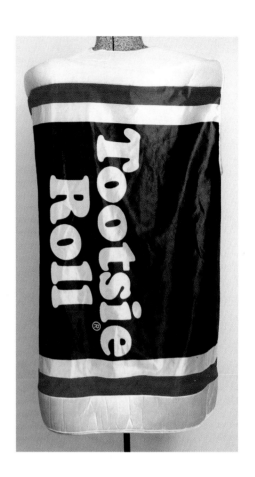

Cartoons, Comics & Animated Television

TWINKLES THE ELEPHANT, 1950s. General Mills; Collegeville. Twinkles the Elephant was the mascot for Twinkles, a sweetened cereal from the 1950s. Value $175-200.

ALFRED E. NEUMAN, 1961. E.C. Comics; Collegeville. "What, Me Worry?" This moron with a missing tooth had actually been a part of Americana since the turn of the century, many decades before MAD magazine became one of the most popular humor periodicals. But starting in the early 1950s, he became the magazine's recognizable mascot with asymmetrical eyes and freckles. Value $300-400.

ANDY PANDA, ca. 1954. Walter Lantz Productions; Collegeville. The cutest cartoon bear on the planet made his debut in the 1939 classic, *Life Begins for Andy Panda*. He would become a regular on the show bearing the name of Lantz's most famous character, Woody Woodpecker. Value $125-150

Below:
ARCHIE, ca. 1969. Archie Comics Publ.; Ben Cooper. The gang from Riverdale High debuted in 1941 ("Pep Comics #2"), but the Halloween costume is modeled after the Archies cartoon series that rocked the kiddies in the late 1960s. The gang even had a #1 hit—the omnipresent "Sugar Sugar." This costume features the clean-cut Archie with his friends, the annoying Reggie and the aw-shucks Jughead, on the suit itself. But Betty, Veronica, Mr. Wetherby and the gang's dog, Hot Dog, are nowhere to be seen. Value $45-55

ALVIN THE CHIPMUNK, early 1960s. Monarch Music Company; Halco. Alvin was the most popular of three falsetto-voiced chipmunks [Simon and Theodore were the other two], a trio who gave grief to the songwriter they lived with, David Seville. A catch-phrase even emerged from the series, Seville's long, anguished cries of, "Allllllllllvvvvviiiinnnnnnnn!!!" Seville's voice was provided by songwriter Ross Bagdarian, who also provided the voices for all three chipmunks. The helium-voiced varmints first became an American sensation in 1958 when the Christmas-themed "The Chipmunk Song" hit #1 on the Billboard charts. Believe it or not, the name "Alvin" was not picked randomly; he was actually named after the vice-president of Liberty Records, Al Bennett. This is an early Chipmunks costume, before they became "cute." Value $125-175

AQUAMAN, 1967. National Periodical; Ben Cooper. Aquaman, "The King of the Seven Seas", dove into our homes for the first time in November of 1941 in *More Fun Comics # 75*. Riding his seahorse, Storm, he fought villains as diverse as the Reptile Men and the evil Black Mantra. The awesome Halloween costume was based on the CBS cartoon that debuted in September of 1967. Value $125-150

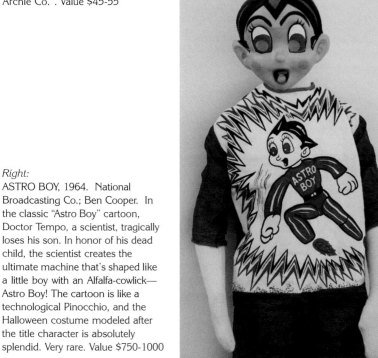

Left:
ASTRAEA, 1977. Filmation; Collegeville. In Greek mythology, Astraea is known as the star maiden, but on the Saturday morning cartoon, *The Space Sentinels* (originally entitled *The Young Sentinels*), she was one of three Greek-named super heroes protecting Earth from a plethora of villains. The show lasted just a year, which means this costume was probably only donned during Halloween 1977. Value $15-25

Below:
ATTACK OF THE KILLER TOMATOES, 1991. Fox Children's Network/Four Square Productions. What began as a purposely-bad movie about vicious vegetables, the cult favorite *Attack of the Killer Tomatoes*, eventually wound up as a cool cartoon in the 1990s. In the animated series, which this marvelously disturbing costume is based on, a mad doctor, Putrid T. Gangreen, sets out to rule the world with his tumultuous tomatoes; trying to stop him are Chad, Tara and their friendly tomato, F.T. Gangreen's voice was provided by John Astin, the man behind Gomez Addams on TV's "The Addams Family." Value $20-25.

ARCHIE, ca. 1977. Ben Cooper. Screened design on vinyl. The box is marked "Copyright 1977, The Archie Co.". Value $45-55

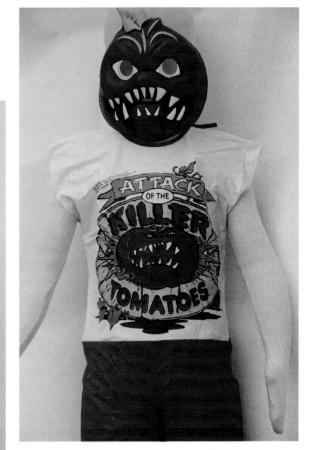

Right:
ASTRO BOY, 1964. National Broadcasting Co.; Ben Cooper. In the classic "Astro Boy" cartoon, Doctor Tempo, a scientist, tragically loses his son. In honor of his dead child, the scientist creates the ultimate machine that's shaped like a little boy with an Alfalfa-cowlick—Astro Boy! The cartoon is like a technological Pinocchio, and the Halloween costume modeled after the title character is absolutely splendid. Very rare. Value $750-1000

ATOM ANT, ca. 1965. Hanna-Barbera; Ben Cooper. "Up and at'em, Atom Ant!" This is one of Hanna-Barbera's more successful mid-sixties characters. He's a mighty mite that saves the world from evil doers like Killer Diller Gorilla and Godzilla Termite in various episodes of *The Atom Ant/Secret Squirrel Show*. Value $75-80

BAILEY'S COMETS, ca. 1975. Ben Cooper. *Bailey's Comets* was an animated television series that ran from 1973 to 1975 and featured the vocal skills of *Scooby Doo's* Don Messick and Frank Welker. Value $35-40

BANANA SPLITS, ca. 1968. Hanna-Barbera; Ben Cooper. The grooviest Saturday morning quartet could be found on NBC with the *Banana Splits*. Who could forget their theme song, better known as "Tra-La-La"? The group included Fleegle, Drooper, Snorky and, as pictured here, Bingo. Bingo, whose voice was provided by the great Daws Butler (Huckleberry Hound, Quick Draw McGraw, even Cap'n Crunch), played the bongos like a hairy Buddy Rich. This is one of the great Halloween costumes of all time, with all four Splits hanging around a pseudo-psychedelic top. And the mask is a perfect rendition of the big-toothed orange ape. Value $75-95

BAMM BAMM, 1971. Hanna-Barbera; Collegeville. Bamm Bamm, the Rubbles' adopted muscle-kid on *The Flintstones*, is a young Hercules who likes to slam down his club and exclaim, "Bamm! Bamm!" He would grow up to play the romantic lead opposite the prettiest girl with a bone in her hair, Pebbles Flintstone, in the 1970s animated series, *Pebbles and Bamm Bamm*. Jay North, better known as Dennis the Menace, provided the voice for the animated adolescent. The costume is modeled after the teenage Bamm Bamm with a mop of blonde hair that makes him look more like Edgar Winter than Bedrock's hunkiest youth. Value $45-55

BATFINK, 1968. Hal Seeger; Ben Cooper. *Batfink*, a classic cartoon from the late 1960s, was obviously a Batman take-off. He, along with his sidekick Karate, helped save the world in their very own Batillac. The costume is adorable, a hard-to-find treasure from a hard-to-remember cartoon. Value $185-225.

BAT GIRL, ca. 1977. DC Comics; Ben Cooper. In the original 1966 *Batman* series, the ever-perky Yvonne Craig played the crime-fighting femme fatale in a bat suit. In the 1997 movie, *Batman and Robin*, the role was filled quite cluelessly by Alicia Silverstone. Value $35-40

BATMAN, 1965. National Periodical; Ben Cooper. In May of 1939, Batman made his debut in *Detective Comics #27*. Second only to Superman in popularity, this Bob Kane/Bill Finger Gotham City crime fighter could boast the greatest, most motley crew of villains imaginable: the Joker, the Penguin, the Riddler and Catwomen to name the main four. Unlike the Man of Steel, Batman had help—from his faithful friend, Robin the Boy

Wonder, and Batgirl. This is the classic Ben Cooper outfit with the amazing Batman logo and a regular Lone Ranger-like mask. In just a year the TV show *Batman* would premiere, and the classic comic character would become utterly camp. Many of the Halloween costumes of this superhero would reflect Adam West's interpretation of the role. This is the last of the Batman costumes before that change. Value $55-65

 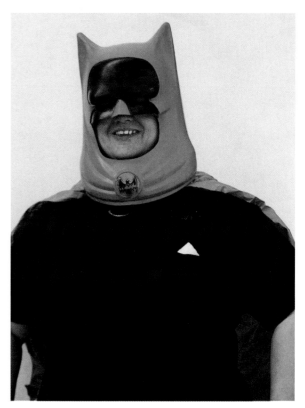

BATMAN, 1966. National Periodical; Ideal. This is more of a toy than a Halloween costume, but it's so beautiful, and some children probably used it for Halloween, that we included it here. This is Ideal's full sized Batman helmet that fits safely over anyone's head. Check out the terrific artwork on the box! Value $175-225

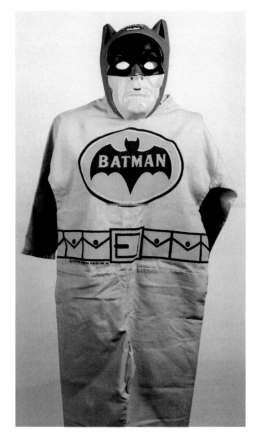

BATMAN, ca. 1974. National Periodical Publications, Inc.; Ben Cooper. A cotton playsuit variation. Value $45-50

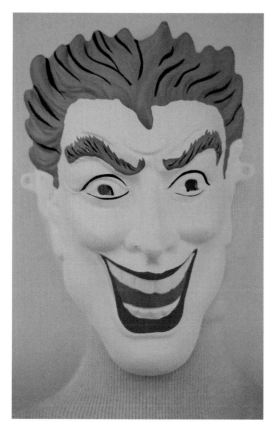

BATMAN'S JOKER, 1966. DC Comics; Pressman Disguise Kit. The Joker was quite possibly Batman's most frightening villain—not the Cesar Romero portrayal from the famed mid-1960s TV show, but the cartoon Joker from the actual *Batman* comics. And this exceptionally rare disguise kit shows how chilling this green-haired albino menace really is. The box art is exquisite, and it comes with a variety of evil Joker accessories. Although technically not a Halloween costume, it is possibly one of the rarest items in the book, a brilliant tribute to that hysterical, giggling gangster of Gotham City. Value $1250-1500.

Left and below:
BATMAN'S RIDDLER, 1966. National Periodical; Pressman Disguise Kit. Although this is not an official Halloween costume, kids obviously used this dress-up kit to go trick-or-treating. It even came complete with "Riddles by the Riddler." In the 1960s TV show, *Batman*, Frank Gorshin played the question-marked villain. This kit is extremely rare, especially complete with its original box. Value $1250-1500.

BATMAN'S JOKER, ca. 1989. National Periodical; Ben Cooper. Batman and several of his enemies were certainly some of Halloween's most popular costumes. Value $25-45

BATMAN'S RIDDLER, ca. 1982. DC Comics; Collegeville. A vinyl costume of Batman's query-riddled enemy. Value $35-40

BEANY, ca. 1960. Bob Clampett; Ben Cooper. Beany Boy, the beanied best friend to a seasick serpent named Cecil, stole the hearts of children across the nation in the 1950s cartoon series, "Beany and Cecil." They actually started as a puppet program, then became one of the great animated shows of TV's first two decades. Value $100-125

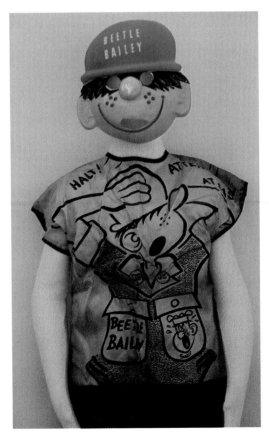

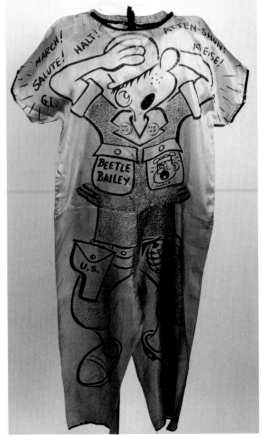

BEETLE BAILEY, 1960s. King Features Syndicate; Ben Cooper. Beetle Bailey, that army mischief-maker whose strip [created by Mort Walker] was one of the big guns on any comics page, makes a wonderfully affable Halloween costume. Two variations of the comic Beetle we all know and love exist—with a picture of his loud-mouth Sarge on the pocket. Value $55-65.

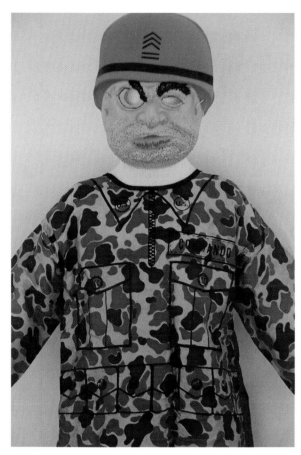

BEETLE BAILEY'S SARGE, 1950s/1960s. King Features Syndicate; Ben Cooper. "Sarge" is none other than Sergeant Orville Snorkel, who made it a point to holler at that goofy GI, Beetle Bailey. The Sarge in this outfit is the original Sarge, before he became Beetle's more benign (and overweight) commander of the last few decades. Value $80-100

BIONIC SIX, ca. 1987. Universal Pictures Company; Ben Cooper. This is the "Jack" costume from the animated series that ran during 1987. Value $25-30

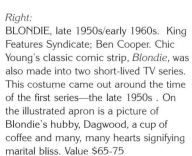

Left:
BIRDMAN, ca. 1967. Hanna-Barbera; Ben Cooper. Birdman was one of Hanna-Barbera's many super heroes to debut in the 1960s, appearing on the program, *Birdman and the Galaxy Trio.* Value $55-60

Right:
BLONDIE, late 1950s/early 1960s. King Features Syndicate; Ben Cooper. Chic Young's classic comic strip, *Blondie,* was also made into two short-lived TV series. This costume came out around the time of the first series—the late 1950s . On the illustrated apron is a picture of Blondie's hubby, Dagwood, a cup of coffee and many, many hearts signifying marital bliss. Value $65-75

Left:
BONES A PART, 1971. Filmation; Ben Cooper. No one was safe around this bundle of bones from *The Groovie Goolies*, especially not Bones A Part himself. Although his name (and hat) is an allusion to Napoleon Bonaparte, Bones was a klutzy, lisping cadaver—usually crashing into a bony heap when he would run into one of the other ghoulish residents of Horrible Hall. His beastly buddy was none other than The Mummy. Value $150-175

Right:
BROOM HILDA, ca. 1976. Chicago Tribune; Ben Cooper. Most Halloween witches were a generic bunch, but not Broom Hilda. Although her face was green, she was hardly a scary monster, especially when flying on her broom with her very own high-IQ vulture, Gaylord. If Broom Hilda's voice sounds familiar, then that's because it was provided by none other than June Foray, better known for providing the voice of Rocky the Flying Squirrel. Value $65-75

BUCKY O'HARE, 1971. Continuity Graphics/Hasbro; Collegeville. Since the Teenage Mutant Ninja Turtles proved so successful, why not a mutant bunny? This one is especially garrulous, a frightening Rambo of a rabbit. Value $10-15

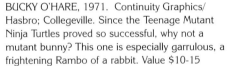

BUCK ROGERS, ca. 1967. Collegeville. A Deluxe rayon costume based upon the famed science fiction comic strip character. Value $125-150

BUGALU, ca. 1968. Collegeville. A rayon costume based on a late-1960s Saturday morning cartoon character. Value $65-75

Left and right:

BUGS BUNNY, ca. 1954. Warner Brothers; Collegeville. The name Bugs Bunny was first mentioned in the 1940 animated short "A Wild Hare." From there, the carrot-chomping critter would spout the immortal catchphrase "What's Up, Doc?" and eventually wind up as the world's most famous rabbit. Starting in the 1940s and continuing for the next sixty years, he would also be one of the most popular Halloween costumes, going through a variety of changes in ear-size and color. But no matter what, everyone would be able to recognize the bunny—easily second only to Mickey Mouse as the world's most famous animated character. This is one of the earliest incarnations of Bugs Bunny for use on October 31st. Value $95-125

BUGS BUNNY, ca. 1982. Warner Brothers; Collegeville. Made of vinyl. Value $25-30

BUGS BUNNY, ca. 1963. Warner Brothers; Collegeville. Compare this costume to the one from a decade or so earlier. Value $50-55

BUGS BUNNY, ca. 1965. Warner Brothers-Seven Arts, Inc.; Collegeville. Screened design on rayon. Value $35-45

BULLWINKLE, ca. 1962. P.A.T. Ward; Ben Cooper. "Rocky, watch me pull a rabbit out of my hat! Ooops—wrong hat." Bullwinkle, that lovable clod of a moose, resided in Frostbite Falls with his best buddy, Rocky J. Squirrel. One of the great cartoons of the 1960s, *The Adventures of Rocky and Bullwinkle* was perhaps the *piece de resistance* of the Jay Ward Studios. The show is still a favorite among children and, mostly, adults. This is an early Bullwinkle costume. Value $100-115

BULLWINKLE, ca. 1968. P.A.T. Ward; Ben Cooper TV Hero. Screened design on rayon with great graphics. Note Bullwinkle's purple/pink antlers on the mask. Value $65-75

Below:
BULLWINKLE, ca. 1973. P.A.T. Ward; Ben Cooper TV Hero. Screened design on vinyl with the same, but slightly bigger and bolder graphics found on the earlier rayon version. Note the yellow antlers on the mask. Value $45-55

BULLWINKLE, ca. 1982. P.A.T. Ward; Collegeville. Screened design on vinyl. Contrast this Collegeville outfit to the previous Ben Cooper versions. Value $45-55

BULLWINKLE, ca. 1971. P.A.T. Ward; Ben Cooper TV Hero. Screened design on rayon copyrighted by Pat Ward. Value $65-75

Left:
BUZZY THE CROW, 1950s. Paramount Pictures Corp.; Collegeville. Part of 1959's "Harveytoons" was this side character, a crow who shared cartoon time with the likes of Owly the Owl, Danny Dinosaur and Finny the Goldfish. The irony of costume collecting is that sometimes minor characters who would be forgotten in a month's time—like Buzzy—would get their own Halloween costume, while major players who are around in re-run heaven forever—like Gilligan—don't.   Value $95-110

Right:
CARE BEARS, ca. 1982. American Greetings; Ben Cooper. Cheer Bear, that ecstatic bruin with a rainbow emanating from his body, was the cuddliest of the "Care Bear" clan. In fact, he's so sweet and lovable that his nose is shaped like a heart!   Value $20-25

Right:
CASPER THE FRIENDLY GHOST, 1960s. Harvey's Famous; Collegeville. Casper, the friendliest ghost you'll know, started on TV in *Matty's Funday Funnies*. Hosting such second bananas as Wendy the Good Little Witch, the Ghostly Trio and Nightmare the Ghost Horse, the show became a pop culture staple, and Casper is certainly the most famous ghost of all time. The Halloween costume is classic Collegeville—with a happy-go-lucky (albino-white) mask and great artwork of a zooming Casper on the suit. Beats a bed sheet with two holes in it anyday! Value $25-$30

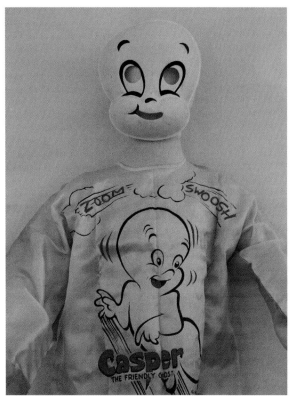

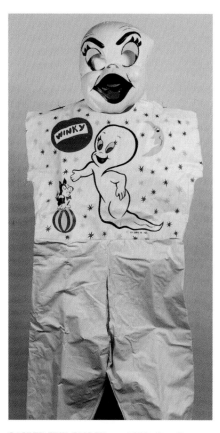

CASPER THE GHOST, ca. 1963. Ben Cooper. Casper? Not really. It is a Casper look-a-like called "Winky" and made by Ben Cooper. The same costume was available marked "Gus The Ghost". Value $5-10

Left:
CASPER THE GHOST'S WENDY THE WITCH, ca. 1977. Harvey Famous Cartoons; Ben Cooper. Screened design on vinyl. Value $35-40

Right:
CECIL THE SEA SERPENT, ca. 1963. Bob Clampett; Ben Cooper. Buddy to Beany on *Beany and Cecil*, Cecil was the world's most famous seasick sea serpent. Cecil's Halloween costume is a grand re-creation of the animated character, complete with red tongue hanging out of the mouth. Value $125-150

CENTURIONS, ca. 1986. Ben Cooper. This is a vinyl "Jake Rockwell" costume from "The Centurions," a short-lived cartoon that appeared in 1986. Value $30-35

COIL MAN, 1967. Hanna-Barbera; Ben Cooper. *The Impossibles* were an animated superhero rock band that included Multi Man, Fluid Man and, pictured here, the mighty Coil Man. Yes, Coil Man could literally spring into action. Because *The Impossibles* only lasted a short time, this costume was only worn for a single Halloween, making it, along with other Impossibles merchandise, rather rare. Value $125-150

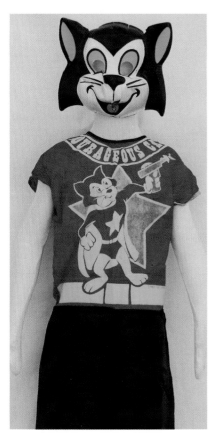

Far left:
COURAGEOUS CAT, early 1960s. Tele Features. Bob Kane, *Batman* creator, came up with his own zoological version of the caped crusader, Courageous Cat and Minute Mouse. The title cat and his rodent companion drove around in their Catmobile, carrying their glue-squirting Catgun. It's quite fun, especially since the satirist was also the creator of the work being satirized. Value $95-125

Left:
DENNIS THE MENACE, 1960. Hall Synd.; Ben Cooper. Dennis Mitchell is simply the brattiest kid who ever got in what's left of Mr. Wilson's hair. The Hank Ketcham comic strip character made a successful leap to the TV screen with the 1959-1963 situation comedy starring Jay North. Aside from his TV and comic fame, the mischievous lad also became the spokesperson for Dairy Queen in the 1970s. The Halloween costume is a marvel, with a cute picture of Dennis and his dog, Ruff, on the outfit. The mask is the best part, with Crunch-berry sized freckles circling the boy's face and plastic hair topped off with Dennis' signature cowlick. Value $55-65

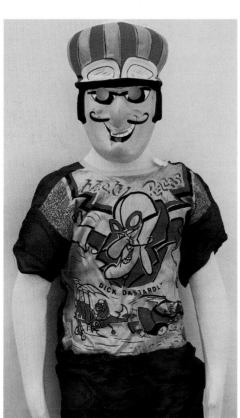

Left:
DICK DASTARDLY, 1969. Hanna-Barbera; Ben Cooper. As the pilot of the wicked Mean Machine in *The Wacky Races*, Dick Dastardly exemplified the melodramatic villains of old. Muttley, his canine companion, snickered whenever one of Dastardly's evil plots inevitably backfired. The costume is a perfect representation of the Hanna-Barbera spoiler, with great illustrations on the suit itself. Value $125-150.

Right:
DICK TRACY, 1963. Chicago Tribune-New York News Syndicate; Ben Cooper. On October 4, 1931, the greatest law enforcement agent to ever hit the comics page debuted: "Dick Tracy." Dick Tracy hosted a slew of terrific villains, like Haf-and-Haf and The Blank. The Halloween costume has to be ranked as a favorite—a fine, realistic mask of the square-jawed hero, his yellow hat, and marvelous artwork on the suit. Plus, his mouth is able to move in a technique that the Ben Cooper studios flaunted whenever they got the chance. Value $95-110

Far left:
DONALD DUCK, ca. 1958. Walt Disney; Ben Cooper. Donald Duck, the world's most famous duck, sported a baseball cap but didn't wear any pants. In the stable of Disney critters, he ranks a remarkable second place to Mickey Mouse. The image on this particular costume is of Donald at the helm of a ship. It came in a tough-to-find "Authentic Walt Disney Character Costume" box. Value $95-110

Left:
DR. DOOM, ca. 1984. Marvel Comics Group; Ben Cooper. Apocalyptic foe to super heroes the world over, Dr. Doom made his first appearance in *The Fantastic Four #5*, "The Prisoners of Dr. Doom." Value $35-40

DUNGEONS AND DRAGONS, ca. 1983. TRS Hobbies; Collegeville. A hard-to-find *Advanced Dungeons & Dragons* vinyl costume, from the 1980s animated series. This is "Evil Fighter", the obvious villain. Value $50-65

DRAC & BELLA, 1971. Filmation; Ben Cooper. Horrible Hall's fanged owner was none other than Count Dracula—Drac—on the wacky *Laugh-In* inspired animated series, *The Groovie Goolies*. Drac's suit includes images of the other residents of Horrible Hall—Frankie, Wolfie, Bella La Ghostly and Bones A Part. Bella also appeared as a costume. Value $150-175 ea.

FARMER ALFALFA, 1950s. Terrytoons; Ben Cooper. Farmer Alfalfa was introduced to the world in 1916, but in the 1950s, on *Barker Bill's Cartoon Show*, the bearded hillbilly in overalls made a comeback. The beloved hillbilly dolt made a marvelous costume, especially the cottony beard. Value $45-50

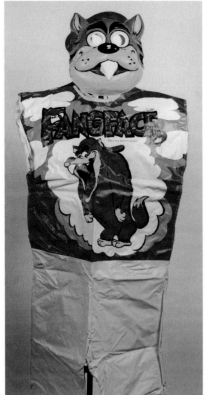

FANGFACE, ca. 1978. Ruby-Spears; Collegeville. The moon is full. Young Sherman Fangsworth has seen it and has suddenly turned into one goofy wolfman. Our furry Fangface drives around in his Wolf Buggy with his friends Kim and Puggsy. The cartoon was on for a year, then became just a segment during the *Plastic-Man Comedy Adventure Show*. Value $45-55

Far left:
ED GRIMLEY, ca. 1988. Hanna-Barbera; Collegeville. One of *Saturday Night Live's* more popular recurring characters, Martin Short's Ed Grimley added "I must say" to the national lexicon. He got his own cartoon series in the late 1980s. Value $15-20

Below:
FELIX THE CAT, 1960s. King Productions; Ben Cooper. Felix the Cat was born in 1919, immediately following World War I and a year before women were designated the right to vote. He would become immeasurably popular in the 1920s, jump strictly to the comics in the next few decades, then find all-new fame on TV sets across the nation in the 1950s. He also made for a spectacular costume. This is the cool Ben Cooper version of the great feline character, with its patented wide eyes and mischievous smile. Value $70-75

Left:
FAT ALBERT, 1977. Bill Cosby; Ben Cooper. "Hey! Hey! Hey!" Fat Albert was the blubbery hero of the famous Saturday morning cartoon, *Fat Albert and the Cosby Kids*, hosted by Bill Cosby. F.A.'s junkyard band usually performed a song at the end of each episode, incorporating a lesson learned in the last half hour. The costume is an awesome representation of the two-ton cartoon star. Value $45-55

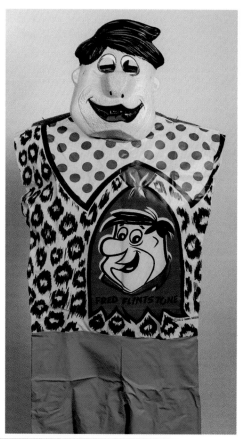

Left:
FRED FLINTSTONE, ca. 1963. Hanna-Barbera; Ben Cooper T.V. Star. "Yabba-Dabba-Doo!" Fred Flintstone—the loud-mouthed patriarch of the Flintstones clan—is one of the most popular Halloween costumes of all time. *The Flintstones*, sort of an animated *Honeymooners* of the prehistoric era, first aired on television on September 30, 1960 and ended on April 1, 1966. It ran as reruns in the 1970s to the present. Value $65-70

Right:
FRED FLINTSTONE, ca. 1973. Hanna-Barbera; Ben Cooper. Screened design on vinyl. Value $25-30

Bottom left:
FRITZ, 1950s. King Features Synd.; Halco. Fritz and his brother, Hans—better known as The Katzenjammer Kids—debuted in the Sunday supplement for *The New York Journal* in 1897. Soon, their animated antics hit the big screen, first in silent flicks, then in sound films under the name *The Captain and the Kids*. In the 1970s, the bratty twosome became part of NBC's ode to the funny papers, "The Fabulous Funnies". Value $95-125

GARBAGE PAIL KIDS, 1985. Topps Chewing Gum Inc.; Collegeville. Garbage Pail Kids were the evil answer to the cutesy Cabbage Patch Kids. Few trick-or-treaters would be caught dead wearing one of the Cabbage Patch Kids costumes, but many would have loved to have gone out on Halloween sporting the outfit to this grotesque Garbage Pail Kid (Michelle Muck), complete with what looks like puke dripping down her face. Value $15-20

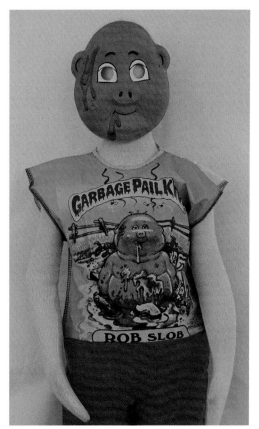

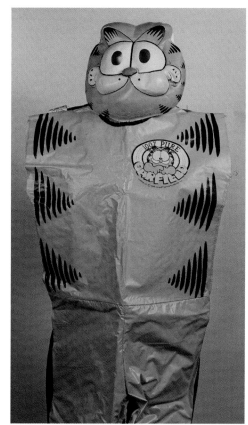

Top left:
GARBAGE PAIL KIDS, 1985. Topps Chewing Gum Inc.; Collegeville. Meet Rob Slob, certainly the most gluttonous and slovenly of the Garbage Pail Kids. Value $15-20

Top right:
GARFIELD, ca. 1989. United Features; Collegeville. The laziest orange cat in the world, Garfield was a curmudgeonly feline addicted to lasagna. He made a popular Halloween costume, especially in the early 1980s when the Jim Davis strip of the same name caught children's—as well as adults'—imagination. Value $25-35

Right:
GHOSTBUSTERS, ca. 1987. Ben Cooper. Screened design on vinyl. After a first excellent movie in 1984 and before a not-so-hot sequel in 1989, a *Ghostbusters* television cartoon series was created. It ran from 1986 to 1991. Someone at the studio may have goofed by not locking up the Ghostbusters name, because a different cartoon beat the Ghostbusters cartoons to television that called itself *The Ghostbusters*. Egon Spengler, shown here, along with Peter Venkman, Winston Zeddemore, Janine Melnitz, Ray Stantz and Slimer became *The Real Ghostbusters* on their animated series. Value $25-35

GARY GNU, ca. 1977. Ben Cooper. Gary was a newscaster on one of the more popular segments of *The Great Space Coaster.* Vinyl costume. Value $65-75

GREEN HORNET, 1966. Greenway Productions; Ben Cooper. Britt Reed was the Green Hornet, the masked crime fighter who debuted in 1936 on the radio. But we all know the superhero from the comics and, especially, the TV series. On TV, Van Williams played the popular Hornet, and his sidekick, Kato, was portrayed by cult icon Bruce Lee. The Halloween costume is highly sought after—by Green Hornet collectors, Halloween collectors, and those who prize 1960s television. Value $175-200

GODZILLA, 1978. Toho Company; Ben Cooper. Originally called Gojira, Godzilla came to life in 1955. Since his classic first movie, he can be found in such sequels as *Godzilla vs. the Smog Monster, Godzilla vs. the Thing, King Kong vs. Godzilla , Destroy All Monsters, Monster Zero,* and *Godzilla 1985.* The big-budget 1998 remake did nothing to enhance this ultimate Japanese monster, a reptilian fire-breather from the Atomic Age. The costume was released the same year as the *Godzilla Power Hour* debuted on NBC. Kids who wore the costume could imagine they were stomping on fake Japanese buildings, breathing fire and crushing everything in sight; the graphics on the suit itself, featuring our flaming nuclear-wasted Saurus, are nothing less than awesome. Value $55-75

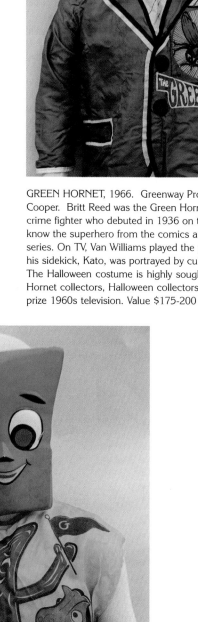

GUMBY, 1967. Lakeside; Ben Cooper. The star of *The Gumby Show* resembles a walking pickle with big eyes and a sweet little smile. He's Gumby, dammit! And when it comes to clay-mated figurines, none are as beloved as this Pokey-riding pop culture touchstone created by Art Clokey. Value $125-150

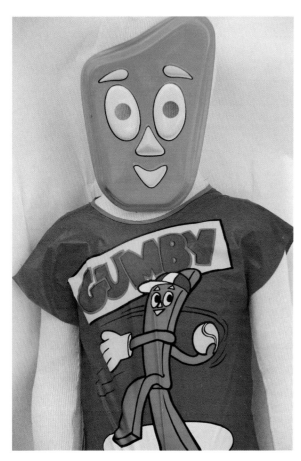

Bottom left:
HAGAR THE HORRIBLE, 1970s. King Features; Collegeville. The famed Viking, Hagar the Horrible, was a comic strip favorite—a red-bearded rogue who could pillage cities but could not dominate his strong Valkyrie wife. The colorful Halloween costume is nothing short of awesome. Value $55-60

Bottom right:
HAIR BEAR, 1971. Hanna-Barbera; Ben Cooper. Welcome to Wonderland Zoo, Cave Block #9. Inside you'll find a band of hairy hippie bears led by the afroed Hair Bear. Our flower child bruin is accompanied by such peace-sign advocates as Bubi Bear and Square Bear. The Establishment is symbolized by the authoritarian head of the zoo, Mr. Peevely. The voice of Hair Bear was provided by Daws Butler, famous for Quick Draw McGraw, Cap'n Crunch, and Yogi Bear. Value $75-95

GUMBY, 1988. Prema Toy Corp.; Ben Cooper. Compare this late 1980s outfit with the earlier version to see what a difference twenty years makes! Value $15-20

GUMMI BEARS, ca. 1986. Ben Cooper. Based on the mid-1980s cartoon series, this vinyl costume models itself after the character Sunny Bear. Value $20-25

HONG KONG PHOOEY, 1975. Hanna-Barbera; Ben Cooper. "Hong Kong Phooey, Number one super guy! Hong Kong Phooey, quicker than the human eye!" Penrod Pooch was nothing more than a klutzy, weakling canine janitor until he would hear of a crime, and then, like a supermutt, would turn into Hong Kong Phooey. Phooey was a karate-chopping superhero that rode around in his Phooeymobile and stopped a myriad of villains. The great Scatman Crothers provided Phooey's voice, while the brilliant Don Messick, most famous for his vocal work as Scooby Doo, was Spot, Phooey's clever cat. Value $35-40

HOT STUFF, 1960s. Illustrated Humor; Collegeville. Hot Stuff was the devilish little star of his own line of Harvey Comics—sort of a Satanic Casper, a red-skinned lad with a pointy tail and horns. There are many generic devil costumes for Halloween (they're almost as abundant as generic witch outfits), but it's always better when children sport a specific character like Hot Stuff. Value $45-50

Right:
HOT WHEELS, 1969. Mattel; Collegeville. Hot Wheels, Mattel's very popular line of toy cars, was also a cartoon that premiered on ABC in 1969. Who could forget its theme song—"Hot Wheels, Hot Wheels, Keep a turnin' now…"? This line of costumes was quite popular with kids who wished to be Al Unser and lasted well into the 1970s. Value $60-75

Far right:
HUGGA BUNCH, ca. 1984. Collegeville. A "Tickles" vinyl costume. Value $20-25

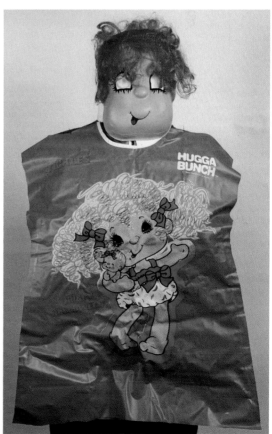

HUCKLEBERRY HOUND, ca. 1967. Hanna-Barbera; Ben Cooper. Huckleberry Hound, a "Clementine"-crooning cartoon canine, became Hanna-Barbera's first major animated star when he debuted in 1958. The "Glitter Glo" costume includes Huck's patented straw hat and polka-dotted bow-tie. Value $45-55.

INSPECTOR CLOUSEAU, 1970. Mirisch-Geoffrey D-F; Ben Cooper. One the most beloved cartoons of the 1960s and 1970s was "The Pink Panther" featuring Henry Mancini's infectious score. Hot on the panther's tale was none other than the bungling Inspector Clouseau, played in the movies by Peter Sellers and on TV (voice only) by Pat Harrington, Jr. Value $55-65.

Right:
IRON MAN, 1966. Marvel Comics Group; Ben Cooper. First appearing in Marvel's *Tales of Suspense* in 1962, Iron Man was the nom de plume of Tony Stark, a rich industrialist who, under his iron gear, fought villains like The Mandarin. The costume is a sight to behold—richly colorful and oh-so-rare. Value $275-325

Far right:
GEORGE JETSON, 1963. Hanna-Barbera; Ben Cooper. Meet George Jetson, the future's answer to Fred Flintstone from the classic 1960s series, *The Jetsons*. The Halloween costume captures Mr. Jetson's rectangular-shaped head, but it makes Elroy and Judy's pa look like he's wearing lipstick. Value $150-175

Right:
JIGGS, 1950s. King Features Syndicate; Halco. From the classic comic strip, *Bringing Up Father*, is this incredible (and incredibly rare) Jiggs outfit. The mask captures Jiggs to a tee—his patented cigar, top hat and pug nose. A glorious reminder of one of the last century's great comic creations. Value $150-175

JANE JETSON, 1963. Hanna-Barbera; Austin Art. She's the glamorous wife of George Jetson, a shopper par excellence on *The Jetsons*. The costume of her far exceeds that of her husband. Look at that suit, complete with an image of Jane with her groovy intergalactic daughter, Judy. But where's Elroy and his dog, Astro? Value $125-$135

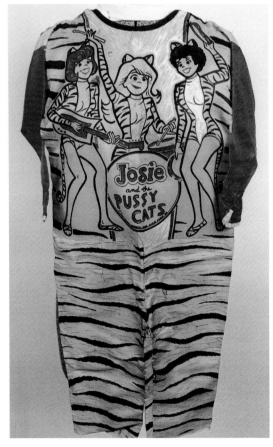

Right:
JOSIE & THE PUSSYCATS, ca. 1971. Hanna-Barbera; Ben Cooper. "Neat, sweet, a groovy song, everybody come long, hurry, hurry…" Josie and the Pussycats are Saturday morning's greatest rock group, leaving the Archies and the animated Beatles in their dust. This cartoon trio—with redhead Josie as the leader—made for a great costume, complete with "ears" for hats! Value $95-125

KATNIP, ca. 1965. Harvey Famous Cartoons; Collegeville. A rayon outfit modeled after the popular cartoon character. Value $95-125

LI'L ABNER, ca. 1963. Capp Enterprises; Halco. Al Capp's hillbilly hero, Li'l Abner, was beau to beautiful Daisy Mae. The overall-donning Duke of Dogpatch [played in the movie and onstage by Peter Palmer] made a gloriously simple Halloween costume. Screened design on rayon with bold black graphics. Value $75-85

LI'L ABNER, ca. 1968. Capp Enterprises; Halco. A variation of the 1963 costume Value $65-75

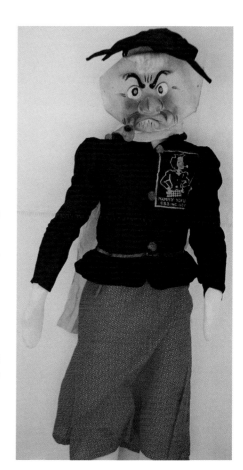

Left:
LI'L ABNER'S DAISY MAE, ca. 1968 Capp Enterprises; Halco. Daisy Mae is the country bumpkin femme fatale of Al Capp's classic comic, *Li'l Abner.* The hottest hillbilly of Dogpatch can be found in this outstanding Halloween costume. The Capp artwork on the suit itself far surpasses the run-of-the-mill mask, although the Halco artists perfectly exaggerate Daisy's luscious ruby red lips. Value $75-80

Right:
LI'L ABNER'S MAMMY YOKUM, ca. 1937. S.S. Inc.; Halco. This is one of the few costumes to come with its very own pipe and a hole in the mask to easily insert it! Mammy Yokum is the toughest of Dogpatch's residents, a hillbilly Lady Justice who will bop anyone who breaks the law with her "good night Irene punch." She makes for one exquisitely odd costume. Value $150-165

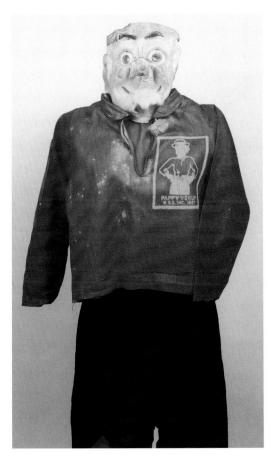

LI'L ABNER'S WOLF GIRL, ca. 1959. Halco. Rebecca wears a rayon costume of the Wolf Girl from the comic strip, Li'l Abner. Wolf Girl was a character that all the men wanted for a girlfriend, but they could never catch her. Value $75-85

LI'L ABNER'S PAPPY YOKUM, ca. 1937. S.S. Inc.; Halco. Pappy was the head of Li'l Abner's family. This two-piece costume is made of cotton and has a starched cloth mask. Value $150-165

Left:
LINUS THE LION, 1965. CBS; Halco. Sheldon Leonard provided the voice for Linus, proud king of the jungle, on the *Linus the Lionhearted* cartoon series. The Halloween costume depicts this cute but ferocious beast, much better than all the generic lion costumes that would prove so popular. Value $125-175

Right:
LITTLE IODINE, ca. 1958. King Features Synd.; Halco. Little Iodine, sort of a female version of Dennis the Menace, was a mischievous urchin who would attach bagpipes to vacuum cleaner bags and litter the sidewalks with "Keep Our City Clean" flyers. The costume is rather rare. Value $145-175.

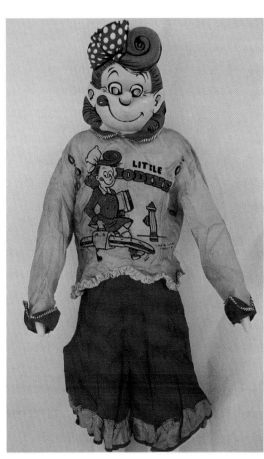

LITTLE LULU, ca. 1978. Western Publishing; Kusan. This Little Lulu looks more like the cartoon character we know and love than the 1950s issue did. In the late 1970s, around the time this costume appeared, Little Lulu could be seen in a live-action after school special and on a new Japanese cartoon. Value $65-70

LITTLE LULU, ca. 1957. MH Buell; Collegeville. Little Lulu began in *The Saturday Evening Post* in 1935, and the girl with the curls became much beloved. In 1956, her cartoon hit TV and the following Halloween, every little girl wanted to venture out as the daydreaming moppet, even if the mask did have an orange face. Value $125-150

Far left and left:
LITTLE ORPHAN ANNIE, 1940s. Famous Artists Syndicate. This is one of the all-time great Halloween costumes. The box shows a bewildered Daddy Warbucks surrounded by multiple dancing Annies. The costume itself is a genuine artifact to a time gone by. Sandy appears twice on Annie's collar, and on her pocket (where the canine says "Arf! Arf!"). In large letters in the center of the suit is the phrase, "Leapin' Lizards It's Little Orphan Annie." The costume even comes with a beret. Little Orphan Annie started as a comic in the 1920s, then emerged as one of the greatest radio shows of the 1930s and 1940s. Other characters from the series included Punjab and the Asp, but it is doubtful a Halloween costume was made for anyone other than America's favorite little orphan, Annie. Value $450-500

LITTLE ORPHAN ANNIE, ca. 1977.
Ben Cooper. Screened design on
vinyl with rayon. Value $25-30

Right:
MAGILLA GORILLA, ca. 1963. Hanna-
Barbera; Ben Cooper. "How much is that
gorilla in the window?" Magilla was an ape
who occupied the window of Mr. Peeble's Pet
Shop in this classic Hanna-Barbera cartoon.
Did you know that the man who played Sam
the Butcher on *The Brady Bunch*—Allan
Melvin—also provided the goofy voice for the
great gorilla? Value $65-70

MANDRAKE THE MAGICIAN, ca. 1957.
King Features Syndicate. *Mandrake the
Magician* debuted in the comics in 1934
and in *King Comics* #1 two years later. Lee
Falk and Phil Davis were the men behind
this amazing character who, with his strong
African sidekick Lothar, kept Depression-era
audiences transfixed. This rayon costume
from the 1950s is very hard to find.
Value $200-250

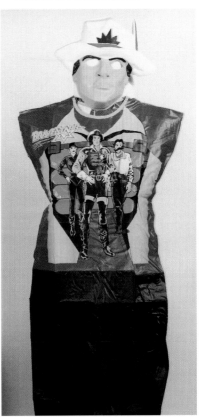

MARSHALL BRAVESTAR, ca. 1982.
Collegeville. The costume is made of vinyl.
Value $35-45

MASTERS OF THE UNIVERSE, ca. 1982. Mattel; Ben Cooper. This is a vinyl costume based on He-Man, the star of the cartoon series *Masters of the Universe* that ran in the early 1980s. Value $25-30

MASTERS OF THE UNIVERSE, ca. 1982. Mattel; Ben Cooper. This is a vinyl costume of Skeletor, a villain in *The Masters of the Universe* cartoon series. Value $25-30

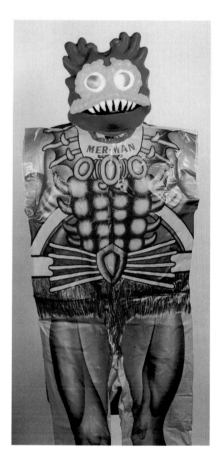

MASTERS OF THE UNIVERSE, ca. 1983. Mattel; Ben Cooper. Mer-Man was one of the cool characters from *Masters of the Universe*. Value $25-30

Left:
MASK, ca. 1982. Ben Cooper, Mask's Matt Trakker is a vinyl costume. Value $25-30

Right:
MICKEY MOUSE, ca. 1931. Walt Disney. This is the earliest Mickey Mouse costume. It includes a body suit with a tail, a hood, a sash and a starched cloth mask and is made of a shiny cotton material. Note that Mickey and Minnie have five fingers and teeth. By 1932, the teeth were gone and the fingers were reduced to three. Value $300-350

Far right:
MICKEY MOUSE, ca. 1958. Walt Disney. Would Mickey Mouse have been as big if Walt Disney had called him by his original name, Mortimer Mouse? According to social historians, Mickey Mouse falls into the category of "The Human Litmus Test"; in other words, if you can't recognize Mickey, then perhaps you are an alien to this world. Easily the most famous fictional character of the 20th Century, Mickey Mouse's humble beginnings start in the 1920s. Who knew then that the big-eared rodent would become a symbol for an entire empire? Value $25-35

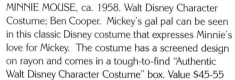

MINNIE MOUSE, ca. 1958. Walt Disney Character Costume; Ben Cooper. Mickey's gal pal can be seen in this classic Disney costume that expresses Minnie's love for Mickey. The costume has a screened design on rayon and comes in a tough-to-find "Authentic Walt Disney Character Costume" box. Value $45-55

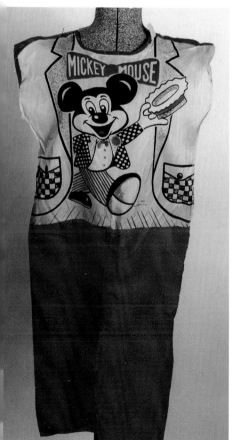

MICKEY MOUSE, ca. 1967. Walt Disney; Ben Cooper Spooktown. This is a rayon costume made for a younger child. Note Mickey's very friendly smile. Value $25-35

MICKEY MOUSE, ca. 1967. Walt Disney; Ben Cooper Spooktown. A rayon costume. Value $25-35

MIGHTY MOUSE, ca. 1958. Terrytoons; Ben Cooper. "Here I come to save the day!" *The Mighty Mouse Playhouse* cartoon series ran from 1955 to 1966. Tom Morrison provided the voice for Superman-like rodent that was constantly saving the girl and foiling the villain. Heckle and Jeckle, two wisecracking crows, were on this cartoon show. This is an all-rayon costume missing the mask and box. Value $75-85

MISTER MAGOO, ca. 1956. U.P.A. Pictures; Halco. Jim Backus supplied the voice of the blind-as-a-bat cartoon hero, Mr. Magoo. The Mister Magoo cartoon strip preceded the television show, which ran in the mid-1960s. Value $125-150

MISTER FANTASTIC,1967. Marvel Comics; Ben Cooper. *In The Fantastic Four*, Mr. Fantastic was actually Reed Richards, but due to a cosmic accident, he became Mr. Fantastic whose skin changed into plastic. Also on hand were the other members of the Fantastic Four—Invisible Girl, The Human Torch and The Thing. Although introduced to the world via comic book in 1961, this costume was obviously based on the cartoon that premiered in 1967. Value $150-175

Right:
MISTER MAGOO, ca. 1962. U.P.A. Pictures; Halco. After providing Mr. Magoo's voice, Jim Backus went on to the challenging role of Thurston Howell on Gilligan's Island. Value $125-130

Far right:
MISTER MAGOO (BICENTEN-NIAL VARIATION), 1976. U.P.A. Pictures; Ben Cooper. Here is a rare Mr. Magoo costume. The Bicentennial variation is a brilliantly colored costume, what Uncle Sam would probably look like if he became a Saturday morning cartoon. Value $40-50.

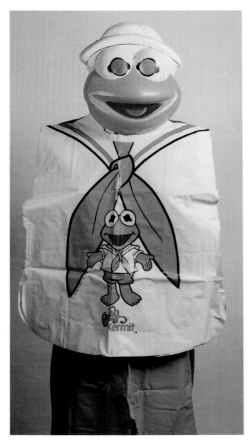

Left:
NANCY, 1971. United Features Synd.; Ben Cooper. Nancy was a dot-eyed smarty-pants in Ernie Bushmiller's classic comic strip, *Nancy and Sluggo*, which began in the late 1940s. The Halloween costume contains scenes from the comic strip, including a politically incorrect moment when Nancy asks for a "dragon bag" instead of a doggie bag at a Chinese restaurant. Value $65-75

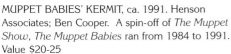

MUPPET BABIES' KERMIT, ca. 1991. Henson Associates; Ben Cooper. A spin-off of *The Muppet Show*, *The Muppet Babies* ran from 1984 to 1991. Value $20-25

Left:
OLIVE OYL, ca. 1961. King Features Synd.; Collegeville. She was the amorous wishbone in the constant battle between Popeye the Sailor and that hairy brute, Bluto. Olive isn't the obvious choice of such violent affection— she was too thin, almost anorexic, with a Pinocchio nose and obnoxious voice. But she made a dandy Halloween costume, with a marvelous picture of Ms. Oyl holding her bundle of joy, Swee'pea. Value $60-70

PEANUTS' CHARLIE BROWN, ca. 1965. United Features Syndicate; Collegeville. Charles Schulz's all-time classic anti-hero, Charlie Brown debuted in *Peanuts* in October of 1950, but it wasn't until the late 1950s and early 1960s that they became a true pop culture phenomenon. A surfeit of Peanuts items hit the store shelves, including (naturally) Halloween costumes. Cool kids went trick-or-treating as Peanuts' great comic Beagle, Snoopy; hot heads would venture out as Lucy; but what kid wanted to proudly roam the streets on October 31st dressed as America's #1 Blockhead, Charlie Brown? In the TV special *It's the Great Pumpkin, Charlie Brown*, our round-headed hero always wound up with a rock! Value $35-45

Below:
PEANUTS' LUCY, ca. 1982. Her full name was Lucy Van Pelt, and she was the know-it-all sister to Linus and the antagonist to Charlie Brown in Charles M. Schulz's *Peanuts*. But for girls who worshipped the comic strip and didn't want to go as the Blockhead, a bird, or a dog, Lucy was their only choice. Costumes had reached a low point at this time, and this is nothing more than a decorated vinyl poncho and mask. The box has good graphics, though. Value $15-20

PEANUTS' SNOOPY, ca. 1982. Probably Bland Charnas. Compare this Snoopy outfit with the 1960s costume. Screened design on vinyl. Value $25-30

PEANUTS SNOOPY, ca. 1965. United Features Synd.; Bland Charnas. Simply put, Snoopy is the most famous Sopwith Camel-flying, Red Baron-hating, bass-playing, novel-scribing, Woodstock-befriending, coconut candy-loathing beagle who ever slept on top of his doghouse. Peanuts' most beloved character, a dreamer dog with a zeppelin honker and sleepy eyes, was given the ultimate honor when the Apollo 10 lunar module was named after him. Cool kids always chose the costume of Snoopy—the one and only Joe Cool. Value $45-55

Right:
PEANUTS WOODSTOCK, ca. 1985. United Features Synd. Woodstock was the cool yellow bird that pals around Snoopy in Charles M. Schultz's much-beloved *Peanuts* comic strip. This simple costume was made of vinyl and created especially for small children. The copyright notice says "1965" but that is the copyright date for the character, not the costume. Value $10-15

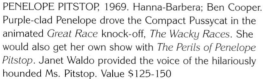

THE PHANTOM, ca. 1960. Johny Gruelle; Collegeville. The classic comic strip of the skull-ringed superhero in a Lone Ranger mask, *The Phantom*, made its debut in 1936. This is a difficult-to-find rayon Phantom costume. Value $125-140

PENELOPE PITSTOP, 1969. Hanna-Barbera; Ben Cooper. Purple-clad Penelope drove the Compact Pussycat in the animated *Great Race* knock-off, *The Wacky Races*. She would also get her own show with *The Perils of Penelope Pitstop*. Janet Waldo provided the voice of the hilariously hounded Ms. Pitstop. Value $125-150

Left:
PINK PANTHER, ca. 1977. United Artists; Ben Cooper. *The Pink Panther* started as a movie starring Peter Sellers, but it's far more famous for its instantly hummable Henri Mancini score. *The Pink Panther* cartoon, which debuted in the 1970s, is the model for this vinyl costume. Value $35-40

Right:
PLASTIC MAN, ca. 1979. D.C. Comics; Ben Cooper. Plasticman, the rubber-armed superhero in a red cape, has been around since 1941 where he premiered in *Police Comics* #1.   But the Halloween costume is based on the jocular 1979 animated series, *The Plastic Man Comedy Adventure Show*, where our hero was known affectionately as Plas. Value $50-55

Left:
POGO, 1969. Walt Kelly; Ben Cooper. "We have met the enemy and he is us." Pogo Possum shared Okefenokee Swamp with the likes of Albert Alligator, Howland Owl and Porky Pine in Walt Kelly's groundbreaking political comic strip, *Pogo*. Pogo, the world's most famous marsupial, wears a red hat in this Halloween costume and actually looks more like Barney Rubble than Okefonokee's biggest star. The comic strip on the suit itself ends with Pogo's alligator pal, Albert, proclaiming, "Being president could be a real head start program." Even as a Halloween costume, Pogo proudly reeks of politics. Value $65-70

Right:
POPEYE, ca. 1954. King Features Syndicate; Collegeville. Popeye's the tattooed sailor man with a pipe and an obsessive craving for spinach. The love of his life is Olive Oyl, and he's always under attack by that bearded brute, Bluto. Popeye, like Fred Flintstone, has so many Halloween costumes and variations modeled after him that it gets overwhelming. Still, he's a magnificent character with many great costumes. This is a very elaborate costume which came with muscles (pinned to the sleeves) for your arms. Value $125-140

POPEYE, ca. 1954. King Features Syndicate; Collegeville. Rebecca wears a similar rayon costume with a plastic mask. Value $75-80

POPEYE, ca. 1957. King Features Syndicate; Collegeville. A deluxe rayon costume with a plastic mask. Popeye has separate starched cloth muscles (pinned to arms). Value $65-75

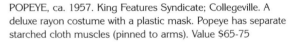

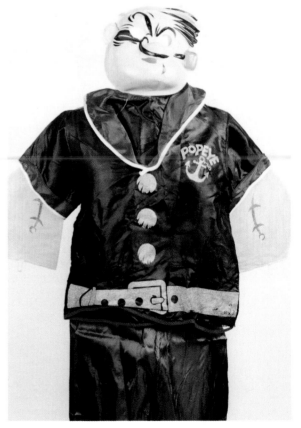

POPEYE, ca. 1961. King Features Syndicate; Collegeville. A standard rayon costume with a plastic mask. Value $65-75

POPEYE, ca. 1965. King Features Syndicate; Collegeville. This is a White For Night Popeye costume with our spinach-eating hero emerging from a television. Screened design on rayon. Value $35-45

POPEYE, ca. 1977. King Features Syndicate; Collegeville. A late-1970s vinyl costume from the classic *Popeye* series. The mask is missing. Value $25-30

Left:
PRINCESS OF POWER, ca. 1985. Ben Cooper. This is the Cat-Ra vinyl costume from the *Princess of Power* animated series.
Value $25-45

Right:
RAT FINK, 1960s. Big Daddy Ed Roth; Collegeville. Rat Fink was Ed Roth's rodent Mr. Hyde in a world full of cute Mickey Mouse Dr. Jeckylls. Roth came up with the deranged rat at a fast-food restaurant in Maywood, California—he wanted to show a friend what Mickey Mouse's ancestors probably would have looked like. Although Rat Fink is a staple of the 1960s, he made a comeback in the early 1990s. The Halloween costume is extraordinarily rare.
Value $450-750

Left:
RAT FINK, ca. 1990. Big Daddy Ed Roth; Collegeville. This is a rare vinyl Rat Fink costume with a full rubber head covering. There was a simple plastic Rat Fink mask that may have originally come with the costume or it may have been available in two versions. This has a great graphic with Halloween flavors mixed in with the marvelous cartoon style of Big Daddy Ed Roth. Value $70-75

RICHIE RICH, ca. 1982. Harvey Features; Ben Cooper. For kids who wanted to be this cute little J. Paul Getty, there was this classic costume modeled after the millionaire tike. Richie Rich began his career in comic books (1956's *Little Dot* #1 was his first appearance), then moved on to cartoons. The *Richie Rich* TV series that this costume is based on began in 1981. Screened design on vinyl. Value $45-55

Above right:
ROAD RUNNER, ca. 1968. Warner Brothers; Collegeville. The Roadrunner first appeared in the movies on September 17, 1949 in a Looney Tunes cartoon entitled "Fast and Furry-Ous". It next appeared as a Merrie Melodies cartoon, entitled "Beep Beep" on May 24, 1952. It continues to run to this day. *The Bugs Bunny/ Road Runner Hour* ran during 1968 about the time this costume was created. This Road Runner mask has a hole where some mom made it easier for her child to breathe. Value $55-65

ROAD RUNNER, ca. 1982. Warner Brothers; Collegeville. This is a vinyl "Road Runner" costume. Value $25-30

ROAD RUNNER'S WILE E. COYOTE, ca. 1972. Warner Brothers; Ben Cooper Famous Faces. Who could ask for a better arch-villain than Wile E. Coyote? All this furry Snidely Whiplash wants to do is catch the Road Runner, that's all. But such a destiny does not come easy—especially when he usually winds up the victim of one of his Rube Goldberg-type contraptions. What kid wanted to be Wile E. Coyote, a perpetual loser in the race to catch the ever-elusive Road Runner? Value $45-55

ROSEY THE ROBOT, 1963. Hanna-Barbera; Ben Cooper. One of the more outstanding costumes ever produced—check out the glorious detail— was of Rosey, the Jetson's robotic maid from that futuristic cartoon series, *The Jetsons*. The nuts-and-bolts housekeeper was sort of a cross between a mechanical Rose Marie and a computer-chipped Roseanne. Value $300-350

SABRINA THE WITCH, ca. 1971. Archie Mdse; Ben Cooper. She started as the sweet-sixteen witch on *The Archies*, then spun-off into various bewitching cartoon series. Her haunting aunts were Hilda and Zelda, and her cat—for you trivia buffs—was named Salem. The costume is mostly rayon. Value $55-75

SCOOBY DOO, ca. 1973. Hanna-Barbera; Ben Cooper. Named after a line from Frank Sinatra's "Strangers in the Night", Scooby-Doo is a cowardly cartoon dog who, with the lily-livered Shaggy, jock Fred, red-headed Daphne and turtleneck-clad Velma, solved ghostly mysteries. Value $35-45

Left:
SEA HAG, ca. 1961. King Features Synd.; Collegeville. The Sea Hag is the witch of the sea, one of Popeye's archenemies. The mask is nothing short of AWESOME, with eyes that flicker like a 3-D picture. While there are many Popeye costumes out there, there are very few of the villainous Sea Hag. Value $150-175

Right:
SECRET SQUIRREL, 1965. Hanna-Barbera; Ben Cooper. Paired with the Peter Lorre-like Morocco Mole was Secret Squirrel (voiced by Mel Blanc), a trench-coated secret agent who fought his enemy, Yellow Pinkie. The costume is a brilliant representation of this Hanna-Barbera character, with grand graphics of our squirrelly spy holding a ray gun. Value $125-140

Left:
SHAGGY, 1970s. Hanna-Barbera; Ben Cooper. Voiced by Casey Kasem, Shaggy is a gawky beatnik in a Maynard G. Krebs goatee whose best friend is a scaredy-cat dog named Scooby-Doo. The costume is extremely rare, probably because all the kids wanted to go trick-or-treating as Scooby and not as his swayback master. Value $50-60

Right:
SHAZZAN, 1967. Hanna-Barbera; Ben Cooper. *Shazzan*, a cartoon about an oversized genie with a Hare Krishna 'do, aired in the golden year of Saturday morning toons, 1967. The Halloween costume is one of the greatest, especially the transparent mask. Value $60-65.

SHRINKIN' VIOLET, 1963. The Funny Company Inc.; Collegeville. One of the motley gang of wholesome kiddies on the classic cartoon *The Funny Company*, Shrinkin' Violet actually shrunk whenever she blushed with embarrassment. This is an exceptionally rare costume from a show now long-forgotten. Value $150-175

SHIRT TALES' RICK THE RACOON, ca. 1982. Hallmark Cards, Inc.; Collegeville. This two-piece Rick the Racoon vinyl costume came from the popular 1980s cartoon series, *Shirt Tales*. Value $20-25

Far left:
THE SIMPSONS, 1989. 20th Century Fox; Ben Cooper Fabric Dress-Up. This Bart Simpson outfit is one of the last Halloween costumes to be sold in a box. Soon after, all Halloween costumes would be sold on hangers. An era suddenly ended. Value $20-25

Left:
SKY COMMANDERS, ca. 1987. Ben Cooper. *Sky Commanders* was a short lived cartoon show that appeared in 1987. Value $30-35

Right:
SMURFS, ca. 1982. Peyo, Licensed by Wallace Bernie & Co.; Ben Cooper Tiny Tots. Believe it or not, those blue nicies, the Smurfs, started in the 1950s, thanks to the Belgian artist Peyo Culliford. Blame Fred Silverman—yes, that Fred Silverman, the TV czar that saved ABC in the 1970s—for the Smurfs' success. Legend has it that he set the stage for the cartoon series after watching his daughter play with a Smurf toy. The rest is history. Value $20-25

SMURFETTE, ca. 1982. Peyo, Licensed by Wallace Bernie & Co.; Ben Cooper. *The Smurfs* was one of the most popular cartoon series of the early 1980s. Smurfette was the lone female in the land of Smurfs. Value $20-25

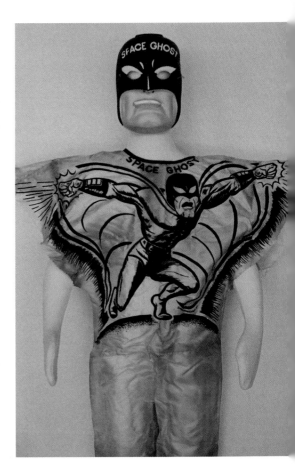

Left:
SNUFFY SMITH, 1961. King Features Synd.; Collegeville. Snuffy Smith was that moronic hillbilly who resided in Hootin' Holler with Loweezy, his wife, and Jughaid, his nephew. The costume is a hoot, with the nose-haired bumpkin wearing his crazy, beat-up hat. Value $65-70.

Right:
SPACE GHOST, 1966. Hanna-Barbera; Ben Cooper. What caped cartoon superhero shot Inviso-power from his Invisi-belt, loaded his wrists with "Power Bands", flew in the Phantom Cruiser, and exclaimed "Great Galaxies!" every chance he could? Space Ghost, that's who—that gung-ho marvel with an executioner's hood and Gary Owens' slick deejay-voice. The costume is an awesome representation of the hero, a character still popular today (thanks to the Cartoon network's hit show, *Space Ghost Coast to Coast).* Value $275-300.

SPIDER-MAN, ca. 1965. Marvel Comics; Ben Cooper. "Spiderman, Spiderman, does whatever a spider can…Spins a web any size, catches thieves just like flies…Look out! There goes the Spiderman!" Spider-Man started out in comic books and moved to TV in 1967 for a series lasting to 1970. He was back again in the 1980s with *Spider-Man and His Amazing Friends.* One of Marvel's greatest super heroes is this red-masked arachnophobia-cure whose costume is usually common to find. The 1960s version is best—with a classic radiating arachnid right there on the breast-plate. Value $125-150

SPIDER-MAN, ca. 1972. Marvel Comics; Ben Cooper. A vinyl variation of the common Spider-Man outfit. Value $35-40

SPIDER-MAN, ca. 1975. Marvel Comics; Ben Cooper. Another variation—the Spider-Man cotton playsuit. Value $35-40

STARCOM, ca. 1985. Collegeville. This vinyl costume is of *Starcom's* swashbuckling hero, Dash. Value $30-35

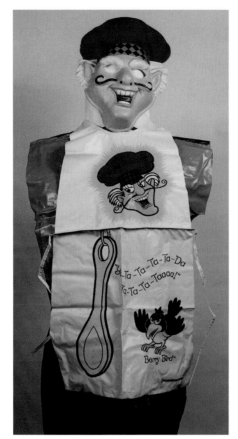

Above center, above right and right:
STRAWBERRY SHORTCAKE, ca. 1981-82. American Greetings; Ben Cooper. Three vinyl costumes based on the *Strawberry Shortcake* cartoon series of the 1980s—"Purple Pie-Man", "Strawberry Shortcake", and "Lemon Meringue". In the land of Strawberry Shortcake, you will find sweet little girls (like Strawberry Shortcake and her friend, Lemon Meringue) and villains that slink through the shadows, turning an otherwise cheery area into a horrible squalor. One of the most wretched Strawberry Shortcake villains is the Purple Pie Man, an evil, mustachioed vermin who wants nothing more than to—gasp!—steal young girls' pies! The costume captures the villain's wickedly laughing mouth; it even features a picture of his compatriot, Berry Bird, on the suit. Value $20-25 ea

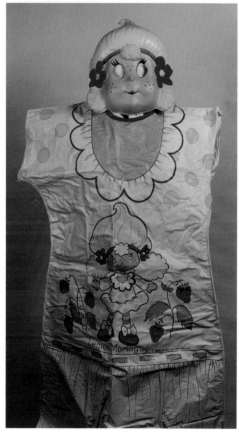

Left:
SUPERMAN, ca. 1973. National Periodical Publications; Ben Cooper. "It's a bird, it's a plane, it's…Superman!" In the June 1938 issue of "Action comics", Jerry Siegel and Joe Shuster introduced Superman to the world. This modern-day Greek God in a red cape would become one of the 20th Century's most indelible icons. No costume exists of Clark Kent, Superman's nervy alter ego, so we have several variations of "the man of steel". In the 1950s, George Reeves chiseled his niche in the world of pop culture playing the world's greatest superhero, and in the 1970s, that honor went to Christopher Reeve. When tallying the fictional characters of the last 100 years, Superman, along with Mickey Mouse and a couple of others, ranks as one of the top five. This is a vinyl costume. Value $25-30

SUPERMAN, ca. 1976. D.C. Comics; Ben Cooper. A Superman costume variation. Value $25-30

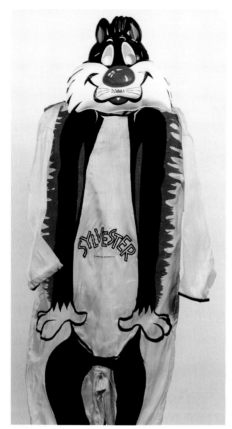

SYLVESTER THE CAT, ca. 1961. Warner Brothers; Collegeville. "I thought I saw a puddy cat!" That "puddy cat" was none other than Sylvester, a feline who couldn't help but spit when he spoke and only wanted to devour little ol' Tweety Bird. The costume is made of rayon. Value $55-60

TOM & JERRY, ca. 1969. MGM; Ben Cooper. Tom the Cat, who starred with Jerry the Mouse in various cartoons, spoke once, and only once. It was in the 1944 cartoon, "Mouse Trouble", in which our Jerry-hunting feline announced, "I don't believe it!" Whenever people use the cliché "cat and mouse," perhaps they could be thinking of these two rambunctious critters, Tom and Jerry. Value $55-60

Right:
THOR, 1966. Marvel Comics; Ben Cooper. Fighting the likes of the Asgards and the Inhumans was the Mighty Thor, a Norse God come to life as a superhero. Too-normal-to-be-true Dr. Blake pounds his magic cane to the floor to become— yes the Mighty Thor. The Halloween costume of Thor ranks second only to Iron Man in superhero coolness. Value $275-325

Right:
TOM & JERRY, ca. 1975. MGM; Ben Cooper. A Tom the Cat variation in 100% vinyl. Value $35-45

TOP CAT; 1960s. Hanna-Barbera; Ben Cooper. Top Cat, better known as T.C., made for one wonderfully goofy outfit, complete with straw hat and tongue hanging out of the mouth. On the box, the creators of "Top Cat", Hanna-Barbera, are actually called "Barbera-Hanna." Value $95-110.

TOM & JERRY, ca. 1989. MGM; Collegeville. Jerry was the quiet mouse, always on the run from that gluttonous cat, Tom. But Tom wasn't the mini-mouse's only partner. Remember Gene Kelly's famous duet with the animated rodent in "Anchor's Aweigh"? Value $25-30

TWEETY BIRD, ca. 1982. Warner Brothers; Collegeville. Tweety was the big-headed yellow bird who was always on the run from that hungry cat, Sylvester. Value $25-30

Left:
UNCLE CREEPY, 1976. Warner Communications; Ben Cooper. Mascot for *Creepy*, this ghoulish relative—along with Cousin Eerie and Vampirella—could be found narrating scary stories in the monthly horror magazine. Value $95-110

Right:
UNDERDOG, ca. 1969. Leonardo TTV; Collegeville. Underdog was the alter ego of lowly Shoeshine Boy, the humble dweeb who, when crisis calls (usually in the guise of Simon Bar Sinister or Riff Raff), turns into that invincible dog wonder. Wally Cox, better known as TV's "Mr. Peepers," provided the voice of both Shoeshine Boy and the heroic Underdog. The *Underdog* cartoon series ran from 1964 to 1973. Value $65-70

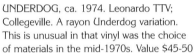

UNDERDOG, ca. 1974. Leonardo TTV; Collegeville. A rayon Underdog variation. This is unusual in that vinyl was the choice of materials in the mid-1970s. Value $45-50

Left:
VOLTRON, ca. 1984. Ben Cooper. Voltron was the "Defender Of The Universe" in a popular 1980s cartoon series. Value $40-45

Above right:
WANDA KAY, 1969. 20th Century Fox; Collegeville. One of the most obscure costumes ever made may be this one, of Wanda Kay Breckenridge, one of Frank and Joe Hardy's friends in the late 1960s *Hardy Boys* cartoons. Actually, it's one of the grooviest costumes ever, with psychedelic swirls and the Hardy Boys guitar logo. And check out those shades! Value $200-250.

Left:
WHERE'S WALDO, ca. 1991. Collegeville. The *Where's Waldo* books featured illustrations with lots of people and things going on, and the goal was to locate the bespectacled Waldo and other items in each picture. Value $25-35

Right:
WINKY DINK, 1950s. Marvel Screen; Halco. Who could forget this classic 1950s mixture of live action and (very primitive) cartooning? Winky Dink was the big-headed, wide-eyed animated tot, sort of a combination (in looks) of Charlie Brown, Rocky the Flying Squirrel and either Eek or Meek (take your pick). (For you trivia buffs, Master Dink's voice was provided by none other than Mae Questel, the voice behind Betty Boop.) Hosted by Jack ("21") Barry, the show is most famous for offering (for fifty cents) "Winky Dink" magic plastic sheets for kids to drape over their TV screens and write on it with their "Winky Dink" magic crayons. The Halloween costume is a hoot—a marvelous re-creation of the beloved Winky Dink (made to resemble the Joker of a deck of cards). A Marvel Screen "Twinky Dink" costume was also created. Value $200-225.

WOLFIE, 1971. Filmation; Ben Cooper. Wolfie was a hyperactive wolfman on the cartoon hit, *The Groovie Goolies*. He cruised the area around Horrible Hall in his very own Wolfwagon, and strummed his guitar to such Goolie hits as "Chick-a-Boom." For trivia masters, Wolfie's pet piranha was named Fido. Value $150-175.

WONDER WOMAN, *see* TELEVISION SHOWS (NON-ANIMATED)

WOODY WOODPECKER, ca. 1956. Walter Lantz. Bugs is the most famous rabbit, Mickey is the world's most popular mouse, and, sure enough, Woody is the world's star woodpecker! Woody was shown to the world for the first time in the 1940 short, "Knock Knock." This is a nice three-piece starched muslin mask, head cover, and jumpsuit. Value $75-85

WOODY WOODPECKER, ca. 1978. Walter Lantz; Ben Cooper. A Woody Woodpecker variation. Screened design on vinyl. Value $25-30

Left:
YOGI BEAR, ca. 1967. Hanna-Barbera; Ben Cooper. "Smarter than the average bear." Sort of an Ed Norton of Jellystone Park, Yogi Bear is only after one thing—picnic baskets! Obviously named after baseball great, Yogi Berra, *Yogi Bear* is just a few short steps behind *The Flintstones* in Hanna-Barbera popularity. This is a rayon "Glitter Glo" costume. Value $50-55

Right:
YOSEMITE SAM, 1970. Warner Brothers; Collegeville. The explosive Yosemite Sam made his debut as a Bugs Bunny antagonist in the 1945 cartoon entitled "Hare Trigger." Value $50-60.

Non-Animated Television Shows

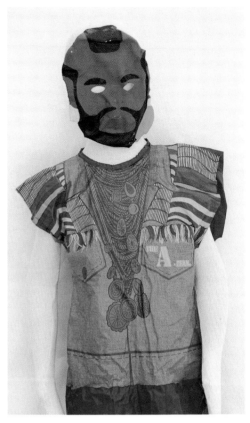

Right:
B.A. BARRACUS, 1983. Stephen J. Cannell Productions; Ben Cooper. Mr. T, the fool-pitying tough guy in a Mandinkan haircut, played the hard-as-nails Barracus in the very successful NBC series, "The A Team." The show centered around a group of Vietnam vets who would help anyone in need. Mr. T's character obviously proved the most popular, and the Halloween costume includes the jewelry that he so famously wore. Without a doubt, this is the only non-pirate costume that a boy, in the early 1980s, would wear that actually sported earrings. Value $10-15

ADDAMS FAMILY; 1964. Filmways; Ben Cooper. "They're creepy and they're kooky, mysterious and spooky, they're altogether ooky, the Addams Family!" Rebecca wears a rayon Morticia Addams costume with a plastic mask. The seductive wife of Gomez Addams was played to eerie heights by Carolyn Jones in the show based on Charles Addams' clever comic. *The Addams Family* debuted on September 18, 1964 and ended its run on September 2, 1966. Value $100-125

ALF, ca. 1986. Alien Productions; Collegeville. ALF stands for "Alien Life Form", and this wisecracking alien, the star of his own situation comedy, took the nation by storm in the mid-1980s. He would eat anything in sight, but he reserved his greatest love for yummy cats. The costume was made in Taiwan and the mask was made in the USA. This was a pretty popular costume and you should not have too much trouble finding one. Value $25-30

Right:
BARETTA, ca. 1976. Tony Baretta, played by Robert Blake, was a low-rent crime fighter who was always getting into the craw of his bosses. The ABC series *Baretta* was a big enough hit to spawn a Halloween costume for the kiddies. The suit is designed to resemble a leather jacket, and it even includes a picture of Baretta's prized pet cockatoo, Fred. Value $35-50

Left:
BARNABAS, 1968. ABC; Ben Cooper. Barnabas Collins, the pained vampire at the "old house" near Collinwood on the ABC "horror soap opera," *Dark Shadows*, had an old-world charm...hundreds of years old, actually. Unearthed by Willy Loomis, Barnabas would become daytime television's most beloved character—possibly the most sympathetic blood-sucker in history. The Halloween costume remains one of the rarest finds—in the top five of the most sought-after character outfits of all time. Value $1250-1500

Right:
BARON BALTHAZAR, 1971. ABC; Ben Cooper. Baron Balthazar was one of the characters on *The Curiosity Shop*, a Sunday morning hit with the kiddies. Value $95-100

BATTLESTAR GALACTICA CYLON WARRIOR; 1978. Universal City; Collegeville. *Battlestar Galactica* ran from 1978 to 1979 and starred Lorne Greene as Commander Adama. The evil Cylons, mechanical menaces in a TV show obviously modeled after *Star Wars*, made a great Halloween costume—they look like Tin Men gone wrong. Value $55-75.

BUCK ROGERS, 1978. Robert C. Dille; Ben Cooper. Gil Gerard played the space adventurer Buck Rogers in the late-1970s *Buck Rogers in the 25th Century* series. Although the show was not a total failure—it lasted 36 episodes and actually received some positive reviews—the Halloween costume obviously wasn't a child's first choice for that all-important trick-or-treat, not in an era of *Star Wars*. Value $50-55

CHUCK BARRIS, 1978. Chuck Barris Productions; Ben Cooper. Chuck Barris was best known for being the smarmy host of *The Gong Show*, an amateur contest where competitors were judged by three pseudo-celebrities and were loudly gonged if they didn't cut the mustard. (The winner got to go home with a whopping $516.32.) The Halloween costume is not as chintzy or as elaborately silly as one might expect, but it does beg the question: What kid wanted to go trick-or-treating as *The Gong Show's* artfully annoying host? Value $35-45

Left:
BIONIC WOMAN, ca. 1976. Universal; Ben Cooper Super Heroes. Like Steve Austin (the Six Million Dollar Man), Jaime Somers (played by Lindsay Wagner) found herself at death's door. [A parachute accident was her undoing.] But she soon was fixed with those clever bionics—in the leg, in an arm and, of course, in her ear. The mask of the Halloween costume is close to capturing Ms. Wagner's features, but what makes it a classic is the suit, which shows our mighty Jaime squeezing something not quite identifiable—is it a board? a sheet of metal? a sandwich?—in her grip. Screened design on vinyl with rayon sleeves and legs. Value $45-55

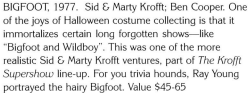

BIGFOOT, 1977. Sid & Marty Krofft; Ben Cooper. One of the joys of Halloween costume collecting is that it immortalizes certain long forgotten shows—like "Bigfoot and Wildboy". This was one of the more realistic Sid & Marty Krofft ventures, part of *The Krofft Supershow* line-up. For you trivia hounds, Ray Young portrayed the hairy Bigfoot. Value $45-65

THE BUGALOOS, 1971. Sid & Marty Krofft; Collegeville. A wacky Saturday morning live-action show, *The Bugaloos* centered on the four-person insect band of the same name—sort of like the Beatles but with antennae and wings. They were hounded by the wicked witch, Benita Bizarre. Value $125-150

THE BRADY BUNCH, 1969. Paramount; Collegeville. When asked what they wanted to be for Halloween, how many of those queried would have answered Greg Brady, guitarist for the Banana Convention and the eldest Brady boy on *The Brady Bunch*? Well, someone must have because there was an actual Greg Brady costume released by Collegeville. Who out there wouldn't agree that, in the Halloween gathering of werewolves and Frankensteins, the scariest costume to be found was, yes, that of Greg Brady? A similar Marcia Brady outfit was also released. Value $100-125

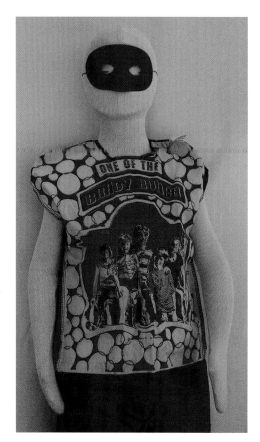

Left:
STEVE CANYON, 1950s. NBC; Halco. The finest pilot of Big Thunder Air Force Base, Steve Canyon started as a comic strip by Milton Caniff in the 1940s and moved to prime time in 1958. The Halloween costume is a fine representation of the helmeted hero, and is not easy to find. Value $75-95

Right:
CAPTAIN KANGAROO, 1959. Keeshan Assoc. Bob Keeshan, who was everyone's favorite Captain Kangaroo, actually once played Clarabelle the Clown on Howdy Doody. But portraying the Captain will always remain his greatest claim to fame. His show was populated with such pop culture luminaries as Mr. Moose, Bunny Rabbit, Mr. Green Jeans, Magic Drawing Board and Dancing Bear, the latter featured on the suit of this phenomenal outfit. Value $85-90

CHARLIE'S ANGELS, 1970s. Spelling-Goldberg; Collegeville. One of TV's ultimate "jiggle" shows, *Charlie's Angels* represents the late 1970s as well as—if not even more than—*Saturday Night Fever*, mood rings and polyester. Three female cops [played in the first season by Kate Jackson, Farrah Fawcett, and Jaclyn Smith] receive various private investigatory assignments from Charlie, a man they never see (voiced by John Forsyth). The Halloween costumes are nothing short of awesome. The Kate Jackson pictured here really resembles the "smart" angel; a costume modeled after Cheryl Ladd (who played Kris after Farrah Fawcett left the series) was also created and really looks like the famed blonde actress. A Farrah Fawcett costume was also released around this time, but not in conjunction with *Charlie's Angels*. Value $55-75

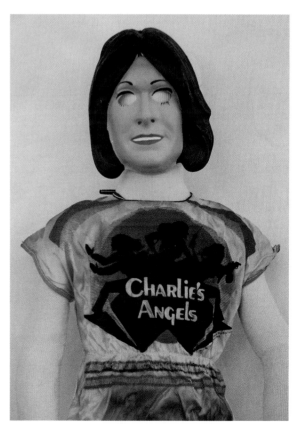

CHACHI, 1982. Paramount; Collegeville. Here is proof that they made a Halloween costume out of even the lamest shows. *Joanie Loves Chachi*, perhaps ranked with *Misfits of Science* as the worst program of the 1980s, spawned this remarkably bizarre outfit. Chachi was portrayed by teen idol Scott Baio, and the mask is an incredible spot-on representation of him. Value $35-40

DANIEL BOONE, 1960s. NBC; Ben Cooper. Fess Parker, who portrayed Davy Crockett in the 1950s, played Daniel Boone, the great pioneer, on the successful *Daniel Boone* TV series (1964–1970). With its prominent coonskin cap, the Halloween costume owes more to the Davy Crockett craze of the 1950s than it does to Daniel Boone (circa 1967). But it's still a fabulous costume, a relic of an innocent TV age long gone. Value $55-65.

COMMANDER KOENIG, 1975. ATV Licensing; Collegeville. Martin Landau portrayed the commander of Moonbase Alpha, which after a nuclear blast, goes careening into space. Most people vote *Space: 1999* as one of the oddest sci-fi programs to air in America. The Halloween mask doesn't really resemble star Martin Landau, but that didn't seem to matter to the two or three kids who actually trick-or-treated as the moonbase officer. Value $55-75.

CONEHEADS, 1970s. Saturday Night Live; NBC. *Saturday Night Live* spawned many popular characters, from the Blues Brothers to the Church Lady, from Wayne's World to The Ladies' Man. By far the most recognizable—with those pointy bald heads—were the Coneheads. This hilarious Conehead mask—a must even today for anyone throwing a Seventies theme party—came complete with "sensor ring." Value $65-75.

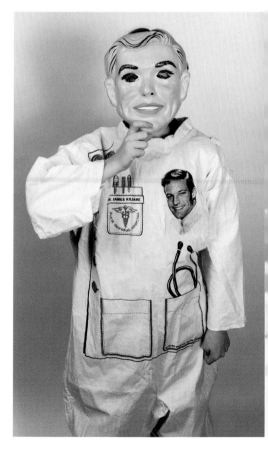

Left:
DAVY CROCKETT, ca. 1955. Walt Disney; Ben Cooper. This costume came with a jacket, short pants, a coonskin cap and belt. Davy Crockett starring Fess Parker was a continuing Disney series that ran in the mid-1950s. Value $145-165

Right:
DR. KILDARE, ca. 1965. MGM; Halco. Richard Chamberlain wasn't a real doctor, but he played one on TV. One of the more popular medical dramas in the middle 1960s, *Dr. Kildare* starred the young Chamberlain as Blair General Hospital's most famous intern. Children didn't have to go in generic doctor garb during the Halloweens when *Dr. Kildare* aired—they could now go as a real-live, albeit fictional, doc. The television show ran from 1961 to 1966. Value $75-85

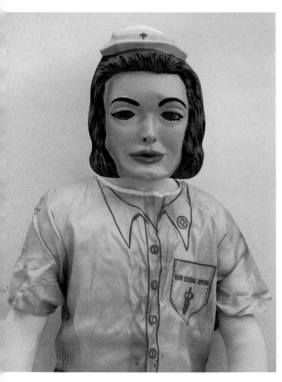

DR. KILDARE'S NURSE, 1965. MGM; Halco. This Halloween costume doesn't make clear exactly which of Dr. Kildare's nurses she is supposed to be—Nurse Lawton (Lee Kurty) or Nurse Fain (Jean Inness)? More difficult to find than the Dr. Kildare outfit. Value $95-125

EASY READER, 1977. Children's Television Workshop; Collegeville. Easy Reader was one of the great characters from the fabulous children's program of the 1970s, *The Electric Company*. And yes, he was played by Morgan Freeman many years before *Driving Miss Daisy, Seven* and *The Shawshank Redemption*. Value $40-65

DUKES OF HAZZARD, 1979. Warner Brothers; Ben Cooper. Although this is obviously a representation of Bo Duke, played by John Schneider, the box only claims that it's one of the *Dukes of Hazzard*. On the suit itself is a grand picture of the Duke Brother's car, the General Lee, and a large version of the confederate flag. Value $25-35

DUKES OF HAZZARD'S BOSS HOGG, ca. 1979. Warner Brothers; Ben Cooper. Jefferson Davis Hogg, better known as "Boss", is the less-than-law-abiding head honcho of Hazzard County on *The Dukes of Hazzard*. So, in the era following Watergate, if kids wanted to trick-or-treat as a corrupt politician, it was probably safer to let them go as a fictional one. This costume, like the general "Dukes of Hazzard" outfit, is one of the few with a re-creation of the confederate flag on it. Value $20-30

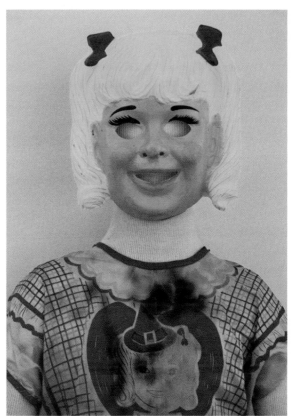

FAMILY AFFAIR'S BUFFY, 1970. Family Affair Co.; Ben Cooper. The character Buffy was so saccharine sweet on *Family Affair* that it was a shock to the country when its young star, Anissa Jones, died of a drug overdose in the mid-1970s. Buffy's Halloween costume includes those cuter-than-cute pigtails and a drawing of her favorite doll, Mrs. Beasley, on the apron. Value $125-150

Left:
FARGO NORTH, 1977. Children's Television Workshop; Collegeville. Another quality costume from that great children's show, *The Electric Company*, which featured the likes of Bill Cosby, Rita Moreno and Morgan Freeman. Fargo was always ready with his secret decoder and crypto-spectometer! Value $40-50

Right:
FLIPPER, 1964. Ivan Tors Films & MGM; Collegeville. Flipper was nothing more than a Lassie of the Sea, and the TV show that bared the dolphin's name was quite popular between 1964–1967. But how many kids wanted to go as the sea-soaked mammal? Obviously a lot because Flipper remains fairly common among Halloween costume collectors. Value $45-75

FLYING NUN, 1967. Screen Gems; Ben Cooper. Elsie Ethrington (played by Sally Field) is a nun with a special ability—she can fly! This bizarre premise lasted a whopping three years on TV. The Halloween costume provided little girls with the opportunity to go trick-or-treating as their favorite teeny-bopper nun. But Ms. Fields' hair was brunette in the show; why does the mask of this nun have blonde hair? Value $95-125

FONZIE, ca. 1976. ABC; Ben Cooper. Arthur Fonzerelli, better known as Fonzie or The Fonz, was the thumb-upping hero of the *Happy Days* gang. And children who sported the leather-jacketed character's costume could pretend they were "cooooool!". *Happy Days* ran from 1974 to 1984, and starred Ron Howard as Richie Cunningham, Tom Bosley as Howard Cunningham, Marion Ross as Marion Cunningham and of course Henry Winkler as The Fonz. Value $25-35

GIRL FROM U.N.C.L.E., ca. 1966. MGM; Halco. A spin off from the *Man From U.N.C.L.E.*, *The Girl From U.N.C.L.E.* starred Stephanie Powers as April Dancer and ran from 1966 to 1967. Value $175-225

Far left:
GRIZZLY ADAMS, 1977. Grizzly Adams Mktg./Shick Sun Classic Prod.; Collegeville. *Grizzly Adams* was a show about a man who escaped the law and headed for nature. Dan Haggerty starred as Grizzly, who befriended Ben, an actual grizzly bear, and hunted and fished. It was directed at the same viewers as *Little House on the Prairie*—but it was not nearly as popular. The Halloween mask is a frighteningly on-target re-creation of Dan Haggerty's gruff face. Value $35-40

Left:
GUNSMOKE'S MISS KITTY, ca. 1956. Halco. Becky wears very rare two-piece decorated rayon costume with a plastic mask. Miss Kitty was the saloonkeeper on the television show, Gunsmoke. Amanda Blake was Miss Kitty, James Arness was Marshal Dillion, Milburn Stone was Doc, Dennis Weaver was Chester, and Burt Reynolds played Quint Asper from1962-1965. The show ran from September 1955 to September 1975. Value $425-450

Right:
HEE HAW, ca. 1976. Youngstreet Pr.; Ben Cooper. The television show *Hee Haw*, starring Roy Clark and Buck Owens, ran from 1969 to 1992. Value $35-55

Far right:
H.R. PUFNSTUF, 1960s. Sid & Marty Krofft; Collegeville. "H.R. Pufnstuf, who's your friend when things get rough…" If *Yellow Submarine* suddenly became a live-action kiddie show, it would look like Sid and Marty Krofft's masterpiece, *H.R. Pufnstuf*. Pufnstuf, a cutesy kid-loving dragon, befriended Jimmy (Jack Wild) on Living Island and protected Jimmy's squealing flute, Freddie. The Halloween costume ranks as one of the all-time greats mainly because Pufnstuf himself is brilliantly bizarre—part Wild Thing from *Where the Wild Things Are*, part Disneyland costumed character, part over-grown child with a Muppet-like head and stringy orange hair. The suit features marvel-ous psychedelic graphics (reminiscent of the show's late-1960s hallucinatory influence) and a perfect mask complete with multi-colored bags under the great dragon's eyes. Value $450-550

Right:
HOWDY DOODY, ca. 1971. NBC; Ben Cooper. Howdy was on in the 1950s but this rayon costume was made in 1971. Value $65-75

Far right:
HULK, ca. 1980. A Ben Cooper Hulk costume. Screened design on vinyl. *The Hulk* was a television show about a scientist (originally Bruce Bannerman in the comics, but the studio executives thought Bruce was too "gay" so they changed it to David Bannerman) whose gamma ray experiments go wrong. Bannerman, played by Bill Bixby, does a Jekyll and Hyde transformation into a powerful green-skinned monster, the Hulk, played by body builder Lou Ferrigno. The Hulk usually destroys lots of property, but does good in the end. The show aired on March 10, 1978 and ended on May 12, 1982. Value $35-45

Below:
I DREAM OF JEANNIE, ca. 1969. Sheldon Leonard; Ben Cooper. *I Dream of Jeannie* made its debut on September 18, 1965, and ended on September 1, 1970. The show starred Barbara Eden as a genie in the bottle, and much has been made of the fact that the TV censors did not want Ms. Eden's navel exposed on the air. Ben Cooper, the makers of this outfit, were one step ahead of the game; there is no opening for a navel anywhere to be found on the costume. Value $55-65

ISIS, ca. 1976. Filmation; Ben Cooper. "Zephyr winds that blow on high, lift me now so I can fly—O Mighty Isis!" So says Andrea Thompson whenever she wants to change into her Egyptian-influenced alter ego, Isis. This live-action Saturday morning show spawned the perfect Halloween costume for girls who wanted to trick-or-treat as a Nerfertiti-laced superhero. Value $25-30

JULIA, ca. 1971. Savannah Prod.; Ben Cooper. The first major black TV character in a non-servant role was "Julia," the title character played by Diahann Carroll. Value $75-95

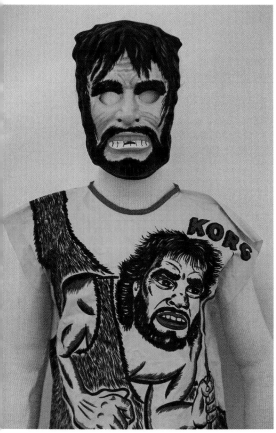
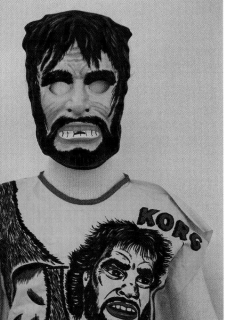

Right:
KUKLA, 1962. Burr Tillstrom; Collegeville. Did you know that "Kukla" is Russian for "Doll"? Well, that Russian word was certainly spoken by boomers who grew up on the 1950s children's show, *Kukla, Fran and Ollie*. Fran was Fran Allison, Ollie was Ollie Dragon and Kukla was the headlining clown-faced puppet with a gargantuan nose. Value $125-$175

Bottom left:
KUNG FU, ca. 1973. A very rare rayon and vinyl costume by Ben Cooper. Kung Fu starred David Carradine as Caine, a Shaolin priest, who avenges the death of his teacher, flees China and comes to America. The vengeful feudal lords of pre-turn of the century China pursue him. Kung Fu ran from 1972 to 1975. (As a bonus, the box has been autographed by David Carradine.) Value $80-95

KORG, 1975. Hanna-Barbera; Ben Cooper. *Korg-70,000 B.C.* lasted only one year and dealt with blue-collar caveman trying to make ends meet during the Stone Age. The costume makes the title character look more beastly than patriarchal, very much like the famed Aurora Cave-man model from the 1960s. Value $35-45

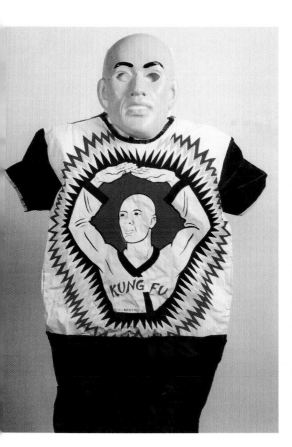

Right:
LAND OF THE GIANTS' GIANT PROFESSOR, 1968. Kent Prod./20th Century Fox; Ben Cooper. Welcome to *Land of the Giants*. When the Spindrift crashes in an unknown land, the occupants soon realize that they are mere Lilliputians in a world of Gulliver's—insect-sized Davids constantly escaping this land of Goliaths. The Halloween costume is one of the greats—where a child's eyeholes can be found in the Giant's mouth. Look at the graphics on the shirt itself; Captain Burton (Gary Conway), his copilot Dan Erikson (Don Marshall) and Val Scott (Deanna Lund) are all hanging from the Giant's shirt pockets or the frame of his glasses. An absolute classic. Also released: a *Land of the Giants* Giant Witch and Giant Cat costume! Value $175-225

LASSIE, ca. 1953. Collegeville. The costume is made of cotton and has a tail and starched cloth mask. Value $145-150

LAND OF THE LOST, 1975. Sid & Marty Krofft; Ben Cooper. Marshall, Will and Holly—on a routine expedition—find themselves lost in a land of dinosaurs. But by far the strangest beings they run into aren't the T-Rex's; they're the Sleestaks. Although this costume is not marked as a "Sleestak", that's obviously who it is. Neither Marshall, Will nor Holly are pictured on the Sleestak suit; that honor goes to Chaka's annoying monkey-like clan. Value $35-45

LAVERNE & SHIRLEY'S LAVERNE, 1977. ABC; Collegeville. *Laverne and Shirley* was the first *Happy Days* spin-off featuring two very funny Milwaukee women—Shirley Feeney (played by Cindy Williams) and loud, nasled Laverne De Fazio (played by Penny Marshall). Value $75-95

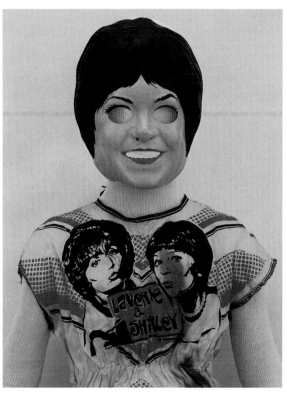

Left:
LAVERNE & SHIRLEY'S SHIRLEY, 1977. ABC; Collegeville. On *Laverne and Shirley*, Shirley was played to comic heights by Cindy Williams. Like Laverne, the Shirley outfit is a perfect representation of the character. But why were no costumes created of the show's greatest duo, Lenny and Squiggy? Value $75-95

Right:
LITTLE HOUSE ON THE PRAIRIE, 1976. Ed Friendly Productions; Ben Cooper. *Little House on the Prairie* ran from 1974 to 1983 and starred Michael Landon. The plot of the show centered on the struggles of a young family living in the prairies of Kansas in the 1870s. This costume is of Laura, a character on the show played by Melissa Gilbert. Value $10-15

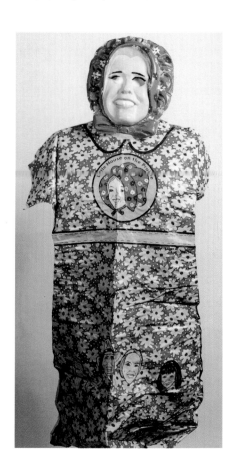

LUCY, late 1950s/early 1960s. Desilu; Halco. Television's most famous redhead, Lucille Ball, helped invent an art form. That's right, her *I Love Lucy* series would be the blueprint for all situation comedies to come. The show's premise was simple: Ball played Lucy Ricardo, wife of Cuban band leader Ricky Ricardo (Desi Arnaz), and all she wanted was to be a part of Ricky's act. In some ways, the show began the era of pop culture, spawning catch phrases—such as "Vitameatavegamin"—and tons of imitators. (In 1953, more people watched the famous episode in which Lucy gave birth to Little Ricky than would watch Eisenhower's inauguration which occurred the following day.) After Ball's stint on TV's greatest show, Lucille Ball starred in *The Lucy Show, Here's Lucy* and 1986's awful *Life with Lucy*. The Halloween costume is not just a rarity, it is one of the Holy Grails of Halloween collecting. Value $300-325

LONE RANGER, ca. 1980. Lone Ranger Television; Ben Cooper. There are various Lone Ranger costumes from the Golden Age of Television. The classic television Lone Ranger show starred Clayton Moore as the Lone Ranger and Jay Silverheels as Tonto, his faithful Indian companion. A television movie appeared in 1956 with these stars and became a series from 1966 to 1969. In 1980, the time of this costume, *The Lone Ranger/Zorro Adventure Hour*, an animated series, appeared on television. Value $45-65

MAN FROM U.N.C.L.E., 1966. MGM; Halco. U.N.C.L.E. stands for United Network Command for Law Enforcement, and Illya Kuryakin (played by David McCallum), the blonde partner of Napoleon Solo, is one of its chief agents. The costume is mid-sixties mod to a tee, especially the swiggly red background behind the secret agent. The mask is unmistakably Kuryakin as well. Value $200-225

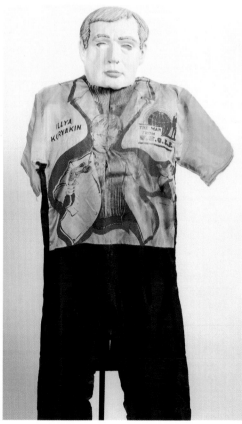

MAN FROM U.N.C.L.E., 1966. MGM; Halco. Robert Vaughn starred as smooth spy Napoleon Solo in *The Man from U.N.C.L.E.,* a clever James Bond-like TV series. The Halloween costume includes the "U.N.C.L.E." logo on the suit, an illustrated gun and a transparent mask molded effectively after Robert Vaughn's face. Value $200-225

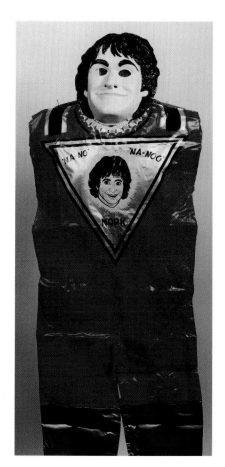

M.A.S.H., ca. 1982. 20th Century Fox; Ben Cooper. TV's most watched program during the Carter years, *M*A*S*H* focused on the doctors and nurses of a Mobile Army Surgical Hospital during the Korean War. The popular series featured an incredible cast with Alan Alda as Hawkeye Pierce, Loretta Swit as Major Houlihan, Gary Burghoff as Radar, McLean Stevenson as Henry Blake, Harry Morgan as Sherman Potter, Jamie Farr as Klinger, Mike Farrell as B.J. Hunnicut, Larry Linville as Frank Burns, and Wayne Rogers as "Trapper" John McIntyre. The show ran from 1972 to 1983. Value $30-45

Above center:
MAVERICK, ca. 1958. A rayon costume with a plastic mask. Maverick televised its first show in 1957 and ran until 1962. The storyline was about two brothers who were gamblers and traveled from town to town in search of the next poker game. The brothers, Brett Maverick (played by James Garner from 1957 to 1960) and Bart Maverick (played by Jack Kelly), had a great sense of humor and the show was a satire of typical westerns of the time. When James Garner left the series, Roger Moore (later of the Saint and James Bond fame) came in as Beau Maverick. Value $65-75

Above right:
MORK, ca. 1980. Paramount; Ben Cooper. *Mork & Mindy* televised its first show on September 14, 1978; the series ended on June 10, 1982. Mork was portrayed by Robin Williams, whose face adorns this mask, and Pam Dawber played Mindy. The plot was that Mork, a friendly, but befuddled alien, landed on Earth and moved in with Mindy. Zany capers followed. Screened design on vinyl with a great image of a young Robin Williams. Value $35-55

Below:
MOUSEKETEER, ca. 1975. Walt Disney; Ben Cooper. *The Mickey Mouse Club* started in the 1950s and is best known for giving a young Annette Funicello her first show biz break. A 1970s incarnation of the Mouseketeers followed and inspired this Halloween costume. Value $30-35

MOUSEKETEER, ca. 1989. Walt Disney; Ben Cooper. Is this modeled after Brittany Spears or Christina Aguilera, Mouseketeers at that time? Value $5-10

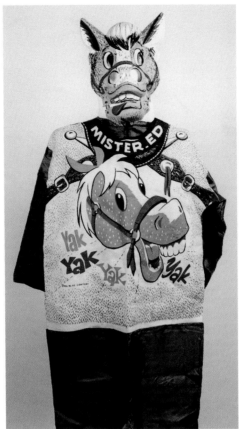

Left:
MR. ED, ca. 1967. Mr. Ed Company; Collegeville. "A horse is a horse, of course, of course…" On the television series *Mr. Ed,* Mr. Ed was TV' s famous talking horse, who spoke only in front of his owner, Wilbur (Alan Young). Mr. Ed's unmistakable voice was provided by Allan "Rocky" Lane. Value $135-150

THE MUNSTERS, 1964. Kayro-Vue Prod.; Ben Cooper. Meet the Munsters. Herman is a Frankenstein-geek; Lily, a witch-haired spook; and Grandpa is a mad scientist vampire. Together, with their children (werewolf Eddie and normal, bland Marilyn), they were *The Munsters*, TV's premiere monster family. Ironically, *The Munsters* premiered the same year as TV's other great horror clan: *The Addams Family*. Lily Munster, played by Yvonne DeCarlo, was the faithful wife to her very own Frankenstein, Herman. She makes a perfect Halloween costume, especially the white streak in her hair. Value $225-250

PEE WEE HERMAN, ca. 1991. Collegeville. *Pee Wee's Playhouse,* starring Pee Wee Herman, was a break from traditional kids shows (it had more in common with the earlier Soupy Sales show with its weird characters and events). The show ran on television from 1986 to 1991. This is a deluxe 100% polyester costume; the standard outfit came on a hanger without a box. Value $55-75

PUNKY BREWSTER, ca. 1985. NBC; Ben Cooper. *Punky Brewster,* starring Soleil Moon Fry, ran on NBC from 1985 to 1989. Value $20-35

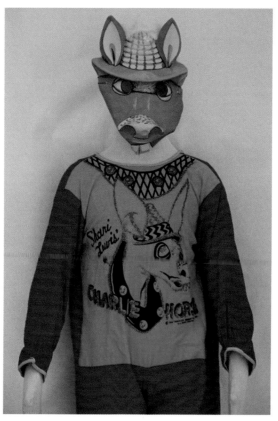

SESEME STREET'S BERT, ca. 1979.
Children's Television Workshop; Ben Cooper.
Sesame Street costumes were popular with the
under five-year-old set. Value $20-25

SHARI LEWIS' CHARLIE HORSE, 1961. Tarcher Productions, Inc.; Halco. Shari Lewis was one of television's
premiere puppeteers with such great characters as
Lambchop and, pictured here, Charlie Horse, the buck-
toothed stallion. The Halloween costume is a gem—with
illustrations on the green breastplate and a phenomenal
pink-faced mask. Value $85-125

Left:
SHARI LEWIS' LAMBCHOP, 1981.
Shari Lewis; Ben Cooper. Lambchop
first appeared on *The Shari Lewis
Show* from 1960 to 1963. Shari Lewis
brought her popular kid's show back in
the 1980s. This vinyl costume was
inspired by the 1980s incarnation of
Lambchop. Value $20-25

SHARI LEWIS' NEVILLE THE DEVIL, ca. 1975. Shari
Lewis; Ben Cooper. A vinyl and rayon costume. Neville
the Devil was a Shari Lewis character. Value $30-35

SIX MILLION DOLLAR MAN, ca. 1975. Universal Studios; Ben Cooper. A cotton playsuit variation of *The Six
Million Dollar Man* outfit. Value $35-40

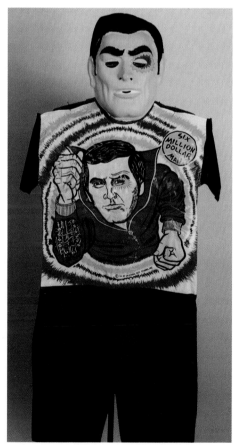

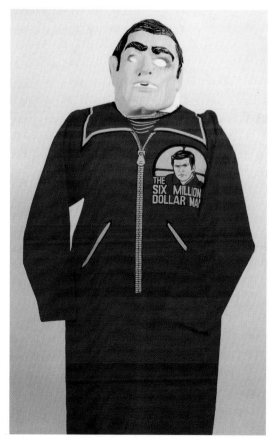

Right:
SIX MILLION DOLLAR MAN, ca. 1974.
Universal; Ben Cooper. *The Six Million
Dollar Man* first aired on television on
January 18, 1974 and played its final
episode on March 6, 1978. Steve Austin
(Lee Majors), after a near-fatal accident,
has been equipped with a bionic eye,
ear, metal legs and arms. He was super
strong and could hear and see a mile
away. He mostly rescued people. A spin-
off of the show, *The Bionic Woman*,
aired soon after and even inspired its
very own Halloween outfit. Value $55-65

LEFT:
SOUPY SALES, 1965. Soupy Sales, WMC; Ben Cooper. Soupy Sales was kind of the Pee Wee Herman of his time—a children's television host who didn't bow down to the lowest common denominator. In fact, he got in much trouble for telling the kiddies to rifle through their mother's purses and Daddy's wallets and send "those little green pieces of paper" that they find to him. The Halloween costume is amazing, including such Soupy staples as White Fang and Black Tooth. Children today wouldn't recognize who Soupy is—judging from the Halloween mask, he looks more like Kevin Spacey. But this costume is a rarity—and a boomer favorite. Value $225-250.

STAR TREK'S MR. SPOCK, ca. 1973. Paramount; Ben Cooper. Screened design on vinyl with rayon legs featuring a great image of a young Leonard Nimoy. Spock is a bit easier to find than Captain Kirk. It is interesting to compare this with the 1967 Collegeville Star Trek costume of the Starship Enterprise's second-in-command. Value $50-60

Above and below:
STAR TREK'S MR. SPOCK, ca. 1967. Desilu; Collegeville. The pointy-eared second-in-command on *Star Trek*, Mr. Spock (played by Leonard Nimoy) is possibly the most loved of the Starship members, which is ironic since he has no emotions, including love. This all rayon Mr. Spock costume was made about 1967 and is extremely difficult to find. Later vinyl and rayon versions of the costume were made featuring Spock and Captain Kirk; it is interesting to compare this early Spock mask with the later versions. Value $95-125

STAR TREK'S KLINGON, ca. 1976. Paramount; Ben Cooper. This early *Star Trek* Klingon costume is harder to find than Captain Kirk or Mr. Spock. Value $75-85

STAR TREK'S CAPTAIN KIRK, ca. 1973. Paramount; Ben Cooper. *Star Trek* needs little introduction. The series started on September 8, 1966 and ended on June 31, 1969. During this time, it was designed to appeal to kids interested in space travel and adventure of the future. Its young audience barely materialized and the show was canceled after only three years. It had, however, appealed to adults, and the flood of letters to the television studio brought it back in the 1970s in reruns and then spin-offs. This costume is a screened design on vinyl with rayon legs and sleeves with a great image of a young William Shatner. It came out after the original series had ended. Value $65-75

STARSKY & HUTCH, ca. 1976. Spelling-Goldberg; Collegeville. These costumes, from the ultimate 1970s cop show, *Starsky and Hutch*, are fine representations of Michael Glaser and David Soul, the actors who portrayed detectives Dave Starsky and Ken Hutchinson. Around the time that this costume was popular, Soul had a #1 hit with *Don't Give Up on Us Baby*. Too bad, though, that Collegeville didn't also make a costume of that *Starsky and Hutch* scene-stealer, Huggy Bear! Value $65-75

Right:
TATTOO, 1978. ABC; Ben Cooper. "Da plane! Da plane!" On *Fantasy Island*, Tattoo, played by Herve Villechaize, was Mr. Roarke's dwarfish sidekick—sort of a mixture of Mini-Me and Tonto. Value $65-75

Far right:
T.H.E. CAT, ca. 1966. NBC; Ben Cooper. A rare costume. This rayon costume is from the cat burglar/spy show that ran on NBC for a short time. The lead character's screen name was T. Hewitt Edward Cat. Value $100-115

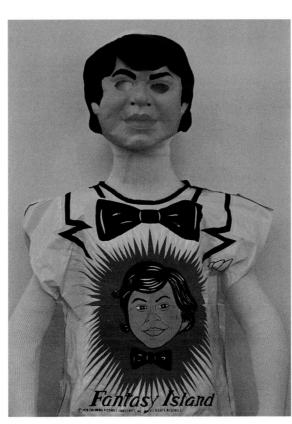

TONTO, ca. 1955. A Halco Tonto rayon costume. The Lone Ranger ran on television from 1949 to 1957. It starred the Lone Ranger, a masked man who fought injustice and used silver bullets. His faithful companion was Tonto, played by Jay Silverheels. Value $85-95

THUNDERBIRDS, 1968. A.P. Films; Ben Cooper. The Thunderbirds were human-like marionettes in the classic children's series set in the year 2063, *The Thunderbirds*. This is an exceedingly hard Halloween costume to find, very rare, which is why its price is so high. Value $325-$350

TWIKI, 1979. Robert C. Dille; Ben Cooper. Buck Rogers' tiny robot assistant on *Buck Rogers in the 25th Century* was actually voiced by Mel Blanc, the vocal talent behind such grand characters as Bugs Bunny and Daffy Duck. Value $30-35

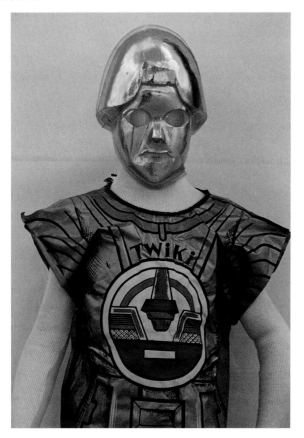

ULTRAMAN, 1971. United Artists; Ben Cooper. *Ultra Man* was sort of Japan's Superman—where an alien named Iota landed on earth and became Ultra Man, fighting off various Godzilla-like monsters. The Godzilla connection seems inevitable since the creator of Godzilla, Eiji Tsuburaya, was also the man behind Ultra Man. Value $150-175.

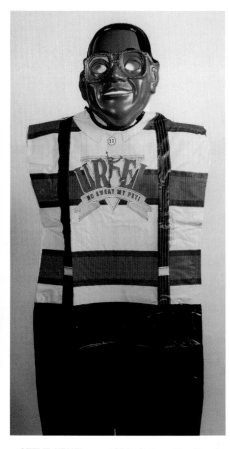

STEVE URKEL, ca. 1992. Collegeville. *Family Matters* ran from 1989 to 1998 and starred Jaleel White as the show's nerd to end all nerds, Steve Urkel. Value $25-30

WITCHIEPOO, 1971. Sid & Marty Krofft; Collegeville. The grooviest witch who ever attacked Living Island, Witchiepoo and her pet vulture, Orson, wreaked havoc on poor Jimmy and his flute on "H.R. Pufnstuf." Billie Hayes portrayed the crazed hag. Value $75-80.

Above center:
WELCOME BACK KOTTER'S BARBARINO, ca. 1976. The Wolper Organization; Collegeville. Barbarino, John Travolta's scene-stealing character on ABC's *Welcome Back Kotter*, was one of the Sweathogs at Buchanan High. (Who could forget his entrance—singing his last name to the tune of The Beach Boys' "Barbara Ann"?) The mask even includes the detail of Travolta's dimpled chin. Value $35-45

Left:
WONDER WOMAN, ca. 1977. DC Comics; Ben Cooper. *Wonder Woman* was one of our favorite television shows. It starred Lynda Carter as Diana Prince/Wonder Woman. She had hypno-tizing blue eyes and the tiniest waist of anyone on television. The show lasted for four seasons (April, 1976 to September, 1979) probably more for Lynda Carter's presence than the less-than-memorable episodes. The Wonder Woman costume is available in several variations. This is a vinyl costume with blue rayon leg panels. Value $45-55

Right:
WONDER WOMAN, ca. 1978. DC Comics; Ben Cooper. A variation of the 1977 Wonder Woman costume. Value $25-30

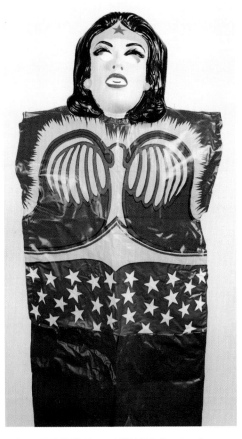

ZEB, 1977. MGM; Ben Cooper. Two characters portrayed by James Arness became Halloween costumes—*Gunsmoke's* Marshall Matt Dillon and Zeb Macahan from *How the West Was Won*. Value $20-25.

WONDER WOMAN, ca. 1987. DC Comics; Ben Cooper. A 1980s vinyl variation of Wonder Woman. Value $25-30

ZORRO, ca. 1958. Walt Disney; Ben Cooper. Zorro originally appeared in the movies—one in 1920 and the classic *The Mask of Zorro* starring Tyrone Powers and Basil Rathbone as the military general. Zorro became a Disney television show starting on October 10, 1957 and ending on July 2, 1959. Four one-hour episodes were broadcast during the 1960-1961 season ending on April 2, 1961. The rayon costume included a hat and ¾-face mask. You had to provide your own sword. Value $125-150

ZORRO, ca. 1962. Walt Disney; Ben Cooper. A cotton variation of the 1958 costume. Value $60-65

Movies

ZORRO, ca. 1965. Walt Disney; Ben Cooper. This costume has a cape and more color than the previous versions of Zorro. Value $60-65

ALIEN; 1979. 20th Century Fox; Ben Cooper. "In Space, No One Can Hear You Scream." So state ads for the most intense film of the 1970s, Ridley Scott's *Alien*. This is also one of the more intense Halloween costumes. In some ways, the Alien creature pictured on the suit looks like the little monster that rips itself out of John Hurt's chest in the movie's most infamous scene. But little kids wouldn't know that as most of them were too young to see this R-rated motion picture. Value $40-60.

Right:
ALIEN 3, ca. 1986. 20th Century Fox; Ben Cooper. This vinyl costume was made at the time of the movie Alien 3, a sequel to the 1979 Alien movie, starring Sigourney Weaver as Ellen Ripley, the Alien fighter. Value $45-55

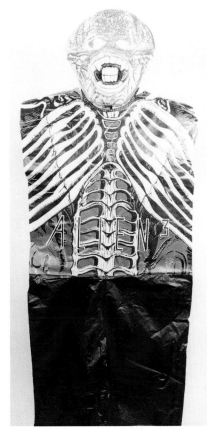

Far right:
ALICE IN WONDERLAND, ca. 1951. Walt Disney. Rebecca wears a rayon and vinyl costume with a starched cloth mask. This Disney animated movie came out in 1951. Several stars with distinctive voices played the characters. Kathryn Beaumont was Alice, Ed Wynn was the Mad Hatter, Jerry Colonna was the March Hare, and Sterling Holloway was the Cheshire Cat. Value $95-105

Left:
BATMAN'S PENGUIN, ca. 1992. DC Comics; Collegeville. The Penguin is one of Batman's chief villains. This particular costume was done in connection with the movie, *Batman Returns*, where the Penguin was played by Danny DeVito. Value $25-40

Right:
CAPTAIN NEMO'S DIVER, 1950s. Walt Disney (?); Ben Cooper. *20,000 Leagues Under the Sea*, based on the Jules Verne classic, is one of Walt Disney's finest live-action motion pictures. The Halloween costume is not modeled after any specific character from the movie, just one of Nemo's faceless divers. Value $45-50

CINDERELLA, ca. 1959. Walt Disney; Collegeville. Cinderella and her coach. Value $45-50

CLEOPATRA, 1960s. Ben Cooper. Although this costume was not licensed by 20th Century Fox, it obviously was inspired by the over-inflated 1963 epic starring Elizabeth Taylor and Richard Burton. Value $20-25.

CINDERELLA, ca. 1968. Walt Disney; Collegeville. A rayon variation. Value $45-50

Left:
CLOSE ENCOUNTERS OF THE THIRD KIND, ca. 1978. Columbia Pictures; Ben Cooper. In the movie *Close Encounters* this alien looks rather sweet, but as a Halloween costume, it is absolutely creepy. You would never know it was supposed to be a benevolent being; it looks more like one of the menacing monsters of the 1950s, *Invaders from Mars* or *The Thing*. That's probably one reason it was so popular. Value $50-55

Below right:
DRACULA, 1960s. Universal; Ben Cooper. "In the annals of living horror one name stands out as the epitome of evil!" So proclaim ads for the ultimate creature of the night, Dracula. The 1931 movie, directed by Tod Browning and starring Bela Lugosi as the Prince of Darkness, spawned numerous imitators, none matching the seductive ghoulishness of the original. This costume, one of many based on the greatest of all vampires, has a fairly negligible mask. But the costume is to die for—the Dracula illustrated on the suit is modeled after Lugosi and not some generic rip-off. And notice how the buttons on his vest are actually skulls. Value $125-150

DOCTOR DOOLITTLE, 1966. 20th Century Fox; Collegeville. Dr. Dolittle could talk to the animals, and the song—from the 1967 Rex Harrison motion picture (inspired by Hugh Lofting's stories)—would go on to win the Academy Award. The costume is one of the greats, with the monolithic top hat and a picture of the Pushmi-Pullyu on the suit. Value $85-125

DOCTOR DOOLITTLE'S PUSHMI-PULLYU, 1966. 20th Century Fox; Collegeville. This is one of the most inventive outfits from the entire history of Halloween costumes. The Pushmi-Pullyu—sort of a Siamese-Twin Llama—was the most interesting creature in the over-inflated *Doctor Dolittle* movie starring Rex Harrison. So a Halloween costume wasn't necessarily a surprise. But the mask—which uses the P-P's double-heads as sort of bunny ears—certainly is. Flip through the hundreds and hundreds of costumes in this book—but can you find one that rivals the cleverness of the Pushmi-Pullyu? Value $95-125

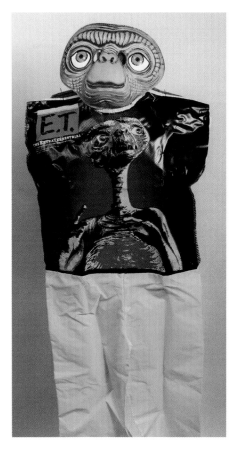

FRANKENSTEIN, ca. 1968. Universal Pictures; Ben Cooper. While writing her great novel *Frankenstein* in the 1800s, did Mary Wollstonecraft Shelly ever dream that she was actually creating one of the great symbols of Halloween? Did she know that Frankenstein's monster would be filmed numerous times in the 20th Century, most famously in 1931 with Colin Clive as Dr. Frankenstein and Boris Karloff as the monster? Did she realize that Ben Cooper's versions of this man-made beast would probably outsell all other costumes celebrating October 31st? Would she have been impressed by the myriad of children who would sport one of these green-faced flat-tops and would extend their arms, stomping their feet as they walk menacingly in imitation of Frankenstein's feared creation? Of course, the answer is that she would not have known what she had wrought with a single novel. But we should be thankful to her; Halloween would go on with or without Frankenstein's monster—but it certainly would not have been as much fun. Value $125-150

E.T. THE EXTRA-TERRESTRIAL, ca. 1982. Universal; Super Star. "E.T. phone home!" This world's most beloved alien made a popular Halloween costume. Every kid, circa 1982, wanted to go trick-or-treating as the wondrous extraterrestrial; unfortunately, the costume didn't include a device to make E.T's neck extend. This was a pretty popular costume, and you should not have too much trouble finding one. Value $25-35

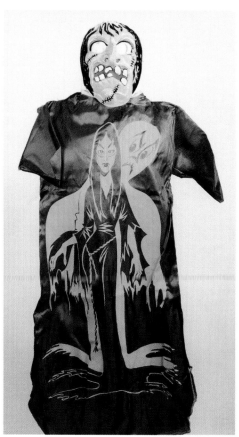

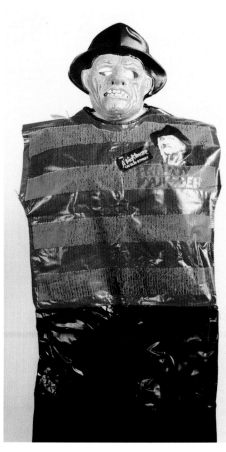

LADY FRANKENSTEIN, ca. 1963. A Lady Frankenstein rayon costume by Bland Charnas. Value $35-40

Left:
FRANKENSTEIN, ca. 1973. Universal; Ben Cooper. A Frankenstein vinyl variation. Value $25-30

FREDDIE KRUEGER, 1987. New Line Cinema; Collegeville. Arguably the most famous villain of the 1980s, Freddy Krueger (played by Robert Englund), entered kids' nightmares in *Nightmare on Elm Street* and its many sequels. A truly frightening invention—his skin was burned off, revealing a hideous smile—Freddy was the model for one of the few quality costumes to come out of the Reagan Era. All the kiddies needed to complete the look was a Krueger glove with spiked fingers. Value $20-25

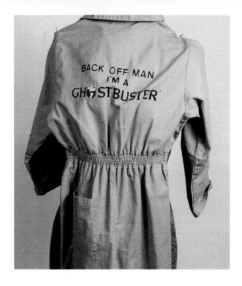

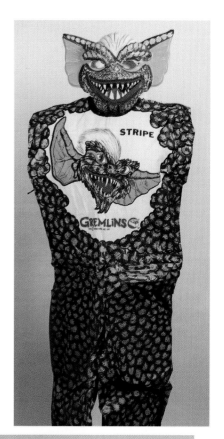

Left & above:
GHOSTBUSTER, ca. 1989. This is a *Ghostbusters II* play suit. Most kids wore theirs on Halloween, but it was not a good seller since the movie was not up to the standards of the first film. The material is a washable cotton. Benjamin has all the fixings to go with the costume. Value $75-85

Right:
GREMLINS, ca. 1984. Warner Brothers; Ben Cooper. The movie *Gremlins* came out in 1984 and was about a boy who got a small furry pet and then broke the rules in caring for it. This costume is of the lead gremlin, Stripe, the mowhawked leader who actually kind of resembled Billy Idol. Kids who were embarrassed to dress as the hero of *Gremlins*, Gizmo, usually chose to go as this slimy critter. Value $40-45

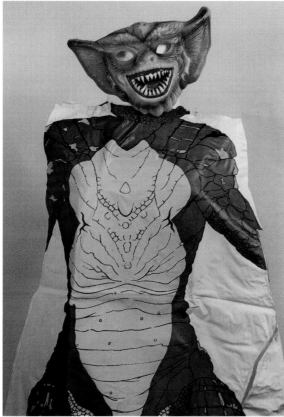

GREMLINS, ca. 1984. Warner Brothers. A pair of Gremlins "Stripe" and "Gizmo" vinyl costumes made in England. These were created as play costumes since England does not actively celebrate Halloween. Value $40-45 the pair

Left:
INDIANA JONES, 1981. Lucas Film Ltd.; Ben Cooper. The whip-wielding Indiana Jones, portrayed with great swashbuckling gusto by Harrison Ford, answers the following question: What do you get when you mix George Lucas with Steven Spielberg? Quite possibly the best movie of 1981 (*Raiders of the Lost Ark*) and one of the great all-time Halloween costumes as well. Value $75-95.

Right:
JAMES BOND, ca. 1979. EON Productions; Super Star. One of pop culture's almighty legends, this Ian Fleming secret agent—007, with a license to kill—makes a splendid costume. Although Sean Connery would be known as the finest James Bond, the Halloween costume is modeled after one of Connery's successors, Roger Moore. And of all the Bond films to make a costume out of, Super Star chose possibly the weakest Bond entry, *Moonraker*. But it was more or less "James Bond meets Star Wars", and the appeal to children helped elevate to trick-or-treat status. Value $65-75

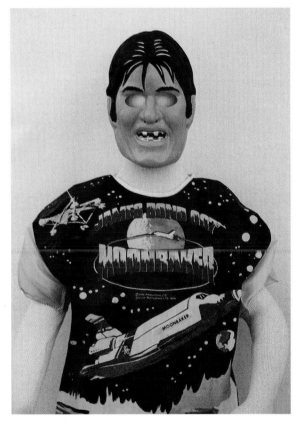

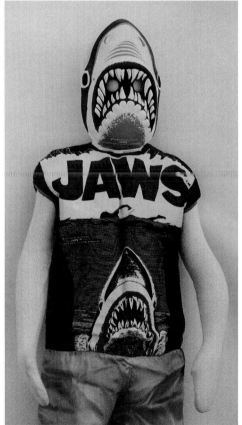

JAWS; 1979. LTD Glidrose, Super Star. He's the menacing metal-mouth who tries in vain to kill Bond, James Bond. Jaws, played by Richard Kiel, appeared first in Roger Moore's finest Bond effort, *The Spy who Loved Me*, and in the worst of the Roger Moore entries, *Moonraker*. The costume of the hulking brace-face is from the latter film. Value $75-85

JAWS, 1975. Universal Pictures; Collegeville. The first summer blockbuster, *Jaws*, the story of a Great White shark terrorizing a small beach community, was directed by a young man named Steven Spielberg. The Halloween costume includes an awesome shark (where the eye-holes are located right in the middle of Jaw's, um, jaws). The one-sheet's catchy image—of a nude swimmer and the giant shark looking up in smiling anticipation of his next meal—adorns the actual costume. Value $45-50

KRULL CYCLOPS, 1983. Columbia Pictures; Super Star. Rell the Cyclops, played by Bernard Bresslaw, was one of the good guys in the 1983 motion picture, *Krull*. The Halloween costume is certainly a hoot—featuring a big eye in the middle of the beast's forehead. Ironically, the child who got to wear this "Cyclops" outfit actually sported a mask with *three* eyes. Is there such a thing as a "Triclops"? Value $35-40

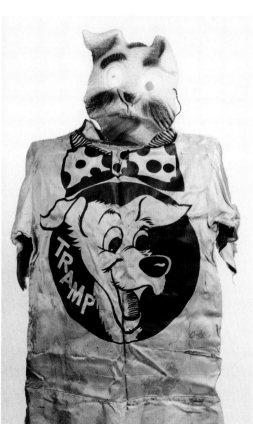

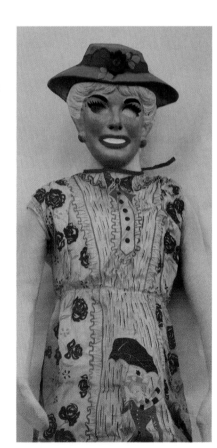

Above left:
KING KONG, ca. 1976. The world's most famous giant ape started his career in the classic 1933 movie (one of moviedom's all-time greats), but the Halloween costume comes from the 1976 remake. The update was directed by John Guillermin, who also directed *The Towering Inferno*. It starred Jessica Lang as Dwan, the girl who Kong is attracted to, and Jeff Bridges as the explorer and hero Jack Prescott. Kong climbs the World Trade Center and is eventually shot down, falling to the pavement below. This is a heavy duty play suit made by Ben Cooper. Value $55-65

Left:
LADY & THE TRAMP, ca. 1958. Walt Disney; Ben Cooper. A rare "Tramp" rayon costume with a starched cloth mask. Lady was the dog star in the animated movie, *Lady and the Tramp*. The costume even has a tail. Value $85-95

Right:
MARY POPPINS, 1972. Walt Disney Prod.; Ben Cooper. "Supercalifragiclisticexpialidouchous!" *Mary Poppins* was easily Disney's finest live-action movie (though it does have animated bits). Sparked by Julie Andrews' Academy-Award winning performance, *Mary Poppins* remains a perennial favorite. And the Halloween costume—with a magnificent illustration of the umbrella-flying Poppins—ranks as one of the best. Value $65-85

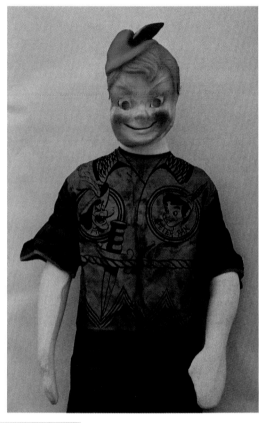

Left:
THE MUMMY, ca. 1965. Universal; Ben Cooper. *The Mummy*, starring Boris Karloff as the 3,000 year-old man (and looking every minute of it!), was released the same year as *Frankenstein* (1932). Mummy sequels include *The Mummy's Curse, The Mummy's Ghost, The Mummy's Hand,* and *The Mummy's Tomb.* More kids dressed up as Frankenstein or Dracula, but enough went trick-or-treating as The Mummy, making the bandaged ghoul Halloween's third most popular monster. Value $100-125

Right:
PETER PAN, 1950s. Walt Disney; Ben Cooper. Peter Pan, that shadow-chasing youth in Never Never Land, made for a great children's outfit from the 1950s. The graphics on the vest of Captain Hook and the Vulcan-eared urchin are beautiful renditions from Disney's animated masterpiece, *Peter Pan.* Value $45-50

PETER PAN'S CAP'N HOOK, ca. 1958. Walt Disney; Ben Cooper. This rare Cap'n Hook rayon costume came with an aluminized cloth headpiece. There probably should have been a mask. The Captain was Peter Pan's nemesis in the Disney movie, *Peter Pan.* Value $120-140

THE PHANTOM OF THE OPERA, 1964. Universal, Ben Cooper. *The Phantom of the Opera* by Gaston Leroux has gone through four film incarnations and a hit Broadway musical. The most distinguished version is also the first—the Lon Chaney horror show with one of the most famous scenes in cinema history: the unmasking of "the phantom". This Universal costume came out two years after the 1962 version (with Herbert Lom as the scarred villain/hero in a mask). The costume is wildly colorful; years later, after children fell in love with Michael Crawford's musical characterization of the Phantom, a half-faced white mask was popular with the trick-or-treat crowd. Value $125-150

Above and left:
PLANET OF THE APES, ca. 1973. 20th Century Fox; Ben Cooper. A group of four-vinyl costumes—Lisa, Caesar, Galen and a Warrior. The first *Planet of the Apes* movie starred Charlton Heston and hit the theaters in 1968. Caesar and Lisa appeared in the 1972 "Apes" sequel, *Conquest of the Planet of the Apes*. In 1974, the movie concept was developed into a short-lived television series. Value $40-65 ea

Right:
ROBOCOP, ca. 1987. A vinyl Robocop costume by Collegeville. Robocop was a 1987 action packed movie starring Peter Weller as a cop who is mortally wounded and rebuilt as part man, part robot. Value $30-45

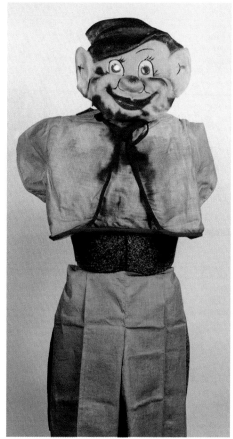

SNOW WHITE & THE SEVEN DWARFS' DOPEY, ca. 1948. A cotton Dopey of the Seven Dwarfs costume. The mask is a starched muslin. This is an early Disney character costume; other early dwarf outfits also exist. Value $145-150

SNOW WHITE & THE SEVEN DWARFS' HAPPY, 1970s. Walt Disney; Ben Cooper. Happy, the peppy dwarf in *Snow White and the Seven Dwarfs*, was a popular outfit (who'd want to go as Grumpy?). As a bonus, the other six little people—Sneezy, Grumpy, Doc, Dopey, Sleepy and Bashful—adorn the suit itself. Value $20-35

Above left:
SNOW WHITE, ca. 1963. Walt Disney's 1937 animated feature *Snow White and the Seven Dwarfs*—the first full-length cartoon—ranks with *The Birth of a Nation* and *The Jazz Singer* as one of the most earth-shattering and influential films of the 20th Century. This particular costume is a screened design on rayon. Snow White is missing her mask and gives no clue as to who made her. Value $35-40

Left:
STAR TREK'S CAPTAIN KIRK, ca. 1982. Paramount; Collegeville. This vinyl costume stems from the 1982 movie *Star Trek: The Wrath of Khan*. Kirk and his crew fight their old nemesis, Khan, played extraordinarily by Ricardo Montalban. Value $60-65

Right:
CATALOG, 1980. Page from the Collegeville catalog showing the Star Wars *Empire Strikes Back* costumes.

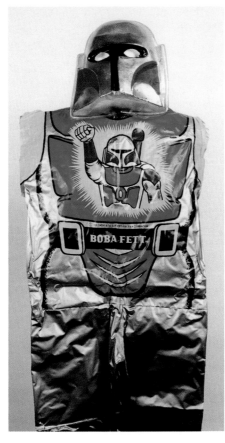

Far left:
STAR WARS ADMIRAL ACKBAR, ca. 1977. Lucas Film Ltd.; Ben Cooper. He's the fish-faced alien from *Return of the Jedi*, one of the good guys who helps the rebels defeat the Empire. He was obviously not a child's first choice for the *Star Wars* character he or she would most like to dress up as (that honor would probably go to Yoda or Chewbacca), which also makes him far more interesting. Also comes in a rare *Revenge of the Jedi* version. Value $20-30. "Revenge" variation $50-75.

Left:
STAR WARS BOBA FETT, ca. 1977. Lucas Film Ltd.; Ben Cooper. He's one of the most mysterious souls in the Star Wars franchise. Boba Fett—a bounty hunter with very few lines, not much to do, but that neverthe-less captured the hearts of twelve year olds everywhere. Value $40-45

Right:
STAR WARS CHEWBACCA, 1977. Lucas Film Ltd.; Ben Cooper. One of the *Star Wars* films' most endear-ing characters is this hairy, eight-foot Wookie. But the costume, quite popular for kids in the late 1970s and early 1980s, looks more like a werewolf knock-off than the Force's furry favorite. Value $30-45

Far right:
STAR WARS C-3PO, ca. 1977. Lucas Film Ltd.; Ben Cooper. Played by Anthony Daniels in *Star Wars* and its sequels, C-3PO is certainly the most talkative droid on the planet. The people at Ben Cooper, possibly unsure whether consumers would recognize the name "C-3PO", called this particular Halloween costume "the Golden Robot." Value $35-45

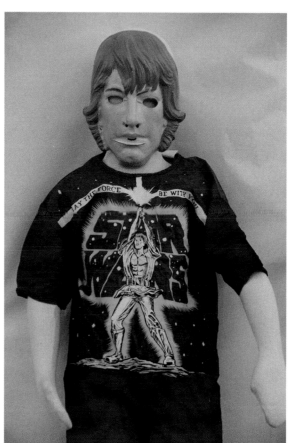

Far right:
STAR WARS LUKE SKYWALKER; 1977. Lucas Film Ltd.; 1977. Luke Skywalker is the hero of the most profitable film franchise in history, *Star Wars*. This costume resembles the fighting pilot Luke, and was popular, but not nearly as popular as that year's chief villain, Darth Vader. Value $30-45

Right:
STAR WARS DARTH VADER, ca. 1977. Lucas Film Ltd.; Ben Cooper. Of all movie villains, perhaps none has captured the imagination of the movie-going public quite the way the evil Darth Vader from *Star Wars* has. And the great thing about the seemingly ubiquitous Halloween costume is that when children got to dress as their favorite black helmeted villain, they ultimately wound up breathing deeply like this master of the dark side of The Force. Value $30-45

Right:
STAR WARS PRINCESS LEIA, ca. 1983, Lucas Film Ltd.; Ben Cooper. She has a double-bunned hairdo and is the only female of consequence in the first three *Star Wars* movies. The mask makes the Princess—played by Carrie Fisher—look rather pudgy and unromantic, certainly unworthy of being Luke's sister, Han's girlfriend, and the only female with the power of The Force. Value $30-45

Far right:
STAR WARS R2-D2; 1977. Lucas Film Ltd.; Ben Cooper. This trashcan-shaped droid burped, beeped and whistled—and became the hero of *Star Wars* and its sequels. Robotic buddy to C-3PO, he's sort of what you get when you mix a trash compactor with a Munchkin. The Halloween costume, on the other hand, is not so nifty. It makes our favorite robot look like a Tin Man reject; only the illustration of our buzzing, bolted buddy is worthy of the great R2-D2. Value $25-30

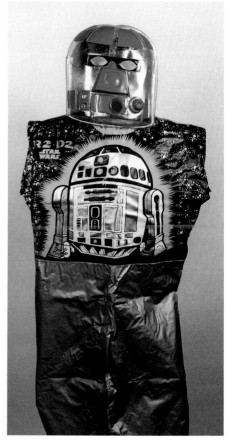

STAR WARS YODA; 1980. Lucas Film Ltd.; 1980. Yoda's sort of the Lee Strasberg of Jedi Knights—a hunched, wrinkled old troll, somewhere between a geriatric gremlin and George Burns. This Frank Oz Muppet appeared in *The Empire Strikes Back, The Return of the Jedi* and, in a much younger version, *Episode 1: The Phantom Menace.* A Yoda mask even captures E.T.'s attention during the Halloween scene in *E.T.: The Extraterrestrial.* Value $40-45.

TIN MAN, 1968. MGM; Ben Cooper. "If I only had a heart!" Originally cast as the Tin Man in *The Wizard of Oz* was Jed Clampett himself, Buddy Ebsen. But Ebsen grew allergic to the silver paint, so Jack Haley took over as the rusty metal man. This is a 1960s incarnation of the Tin Man. Check out the marvelous *Wizard of Oz* cartoon images of the Tin Man and the Wizard on the suit. Value $85-95.

STAR WARS WICKET, ca. 1983. Lucas Film Ltd.; Ben Cooper. Wicket was the most famous of the fuzz-ball Teddy Bear warriors known as the Ewoks from the third *Star Wars* chapter, *Return of the Jedi.* Value $40-45

THIS ISLAND EARTH, 1980. Universal; Collegeville. This is obviously modeled after the mutant monster from the classic 1955 motion picture, *This Island Earth.* But all the box says is "Mutant." Value $45-55

Far left:
V.I.N.C.E.N.T., 1979. Walt Disney Prod.; Ben Cooper. From Disney's first PG-rated motion picture, *The Black Hole*. V.I.N.C.E.N.T. was sort of a cutesy version of R2-D2 that performed a task even the great *Star Wars* droid couldn't—he could fly. Value 65-85.

Left:
WIZARD OF OZ, WICKED WITCH OF THE WEST, ca. 1967. Unknown. Kaitlin wears a unusual rayon costume showing the Wicked Witch of the West terrorizing the Munchkins. The design is done in glitter Value $55-65

THE WOLFMAN, 1970s. Universal; Collegeville. "Even the man who is pure of heart and says his prayers every night may become a wolf when the wolf bane bloom…" Lon Chaney, Jr. made a name for himself by portraying Lawrence Talbot, the human-turned-wolf in various Universal features, who could only be stopped by a silver bullet. Right up there with Frankenstein, Dracula, and the Mummy, he remains a Halloween staple, with more generic outfits than any of his fellow famous monsters, save for Dracula. Value $125-175

WILLOW, ca. 1988. Lucas Films Ltd.; Ben Cooper. *Willow* was a 1988 movie directed by Ron Howard. Value $25-45

Personalities, Professions & People

Left and below:
BEATLES, ca. 1960s. Nems Entertainment Ltd.; Ben Cooper. One of the great Halloween costumes belongs to the Fab Four, those Liverpudlian pop masters who took over the music world in the 1960s—the Beatles. All four Beatles were created by Ben Cooper, the hardest costume to obtain being John. The Beatles started as the Quarrymen, before changing their name to the Silver Beatles and then just the Beatles. In 1964, on the *Ed Sullivan Show*, they became the most successful rock band of the century. They had more #1 singles than any other artist, including Elvis. And their influence can still be felt. These costumes were designed for Halloween, 1964, when any hip youngster—boy or girl—wanted to trick-or-treat as John, Paul, George, or Ringo. The costumes of the Moptops are easily some of the most sought-after Halloween outfits of them all, and to have a full set means that you stand apart from most other Beatles collectors. Value: Set of four, $2500-3000. Individual Value: John, $550-650. Paul, $500-600. George, $500-600. Ringo, $500-600.

YELLOW SUBMARINE, 1968. King Features Subafilms; Collegeville. The Beatles appear on the fabulous suit of this rare costume. The mask is of a dreaded Blue Meany—the Beatles' foe in the very successful Peter Max-inspired animated movie. Sharing space with the Fab Four on the costume is a Butterfly Stomper, two Apple Bonkers, Jeremy Hillary Boob Phd., and, yes, the Yellow Submarine itself. *Yellow Submarine* marks the first time that a movie was actually inspired by a pop song, and the Halloween costume rivals H.R. Pufnstuf as the ultimate in groovy Halloween psychedelia. Value $750-950. A mint example has sold for $2440.

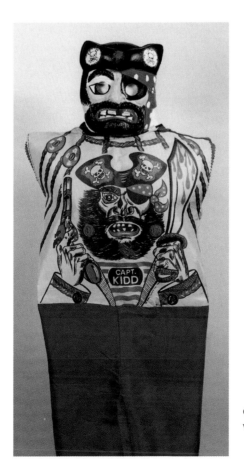

CAPTAIN KIDD, ca. 1963. A rayon costume with a plastic mask. Value $35-45

125

CAVE MAN, ca. 1974. Ben Cooper. A Dino-Rama Caveman rayon and vinyl costume. Value $25-30

CONFEDERATE SOLDIER, ca. 1961. Collegeville. A difficult-to-find Confederate Soldier rayon costume. The American Civil War (or War Between the States) centennial was celebrated from 1961 to 1965. There probably was a matching Union Soldier costume. Value $75-95

Right:
DRUM MAJOR, ca. 1960, Ben Cooper An all rayon costume. Value $30-40

Left:
DR. JEKYLL & MR. HYDE, ca. 1952. Ben Cooper Spotlite. A very rare Dr. Jeckyll and Mr. Hyde rayon and vinyl costume with a starched cloth two-faced mask. Some of the early 1950s costumes used a vinyl material that has held up very well over the years. Value $225-250

Right:
EVEL KNIEVEL, ca. 1974. Evel Knievel; Ben Cooper. America's #1 daredevil was immortalized for Halloweens with this incredible costume, and he was at the pinnacle of his success when it was released in 1974. Evel gained notoriety by jumping his motorcycle over buses, cars, and eventually the Snake River. He retired after he had broken most of the bones in his body. I imagine that every kid that wore this costume rode his "Stingray" bike out while trick-or-treating. Value $50-55

Far right:
FARRAH FAWCETT, ca. 1977. Collegeville. Farrah, possibly Charlie's most famous angel (she played Jill Munroe and sported one of the oft-imitated hairstyles of all time), only lasted one season on that great jiggle-fest. This outfit was not part of the *Charlie's Angels* line; it was solely a Farrah affair. Value $55-65

HER ROYAL HIGHNESS, THE QUEEN, ca. 1958. Ben Cooper. A very rare Her Royal Highness Queen rayon costume with a decorated cardboard tiara. Value $80-85

FIREMAN, ca. 1975. Collegeville. A vinyl "Emergency Fireman" costume. Value $15-20

FOOTBALL, ca. 1982. Collegeville. A "Sportfreak Football" vinyl costume. Value $30-35

JAIL BIRD, ca. 1934. A great early Jail Bird costume in remarkable condition. No maker information on this commercially made cotton three piece costume. Value $175-200

JOHNNY TREMAIN, ca. 1958. Walt Disney; Ben Cooper. A very rare rayon costume. Johnny Tremain was a Disney television character who embodied the patriotic spirit of the Revolutionary War Minutemen. Value $75-100

THE KENNEDYS, 1963. Ben Cooper. Before his assassination, John F. Kennedy, the youngest elected President of the United States, was ridiculed in packs of joke cards and, yes, in Halloween costumes. Although the costume is only entitled "Mr. President," it is most certainly JFK (and even includes the initials "JFK" on the pocket). As for the First Lady, though it's not labeled "Jackie Kennedy", it is obviously inspired by the future Jackie O. (it looks just like her!). Unfortunately, there is no pillbox hat. Value for each $95-125.

Below:

KISS, ca. 1977. Aucoin Management; Collegeville. Kiss, the painted-face rock band, merged heavy metal with glitter—lots of leather, lots of concert blood, lots of pre-pubescent fans. But their make-up will always be more famous than their music. Kids sporting one of their Halloween costumes probably enhanced the look by carrying around an electric guitar and spewing out Kiss classics like "Shout It Out Loud" or "Black Diamond." There were four members of Kiss: Gene Simmons, Paul Stanley, Ace Frehley and Peter Criss. Of course Gene is the best of the costumes—mainly because it comes complete with his pointy serpent-tongue emerging from his opened mouth. The costumes came in two variations—one with real hair, the other with mere plastic. For the cool kids on the block, either version was a must. Value for each (with hair): $125-$150. Value for each (plastic hair): $100-$125. Value Set of four (real hair): $550-650. Value Set of four (plastic hair): $450-550.

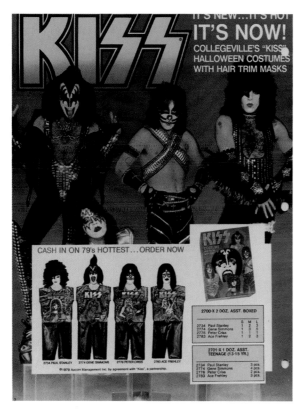

CATALOG, 1977. Page from the Collegeville catalog featuring the Kiss costumes.

Below:
LAUREL & HARDY, 1966. Larry Harmon Picture Corp.; Ben Cooper. Here is one of the all-time great Halloween costumes with a two-faced mask modeled after the great comedy team, Laurel and Hardy. Compare it to the Halco Oliver Hardy costume (also pictured) released around the same time period. Values: Laurel & Hardy (Ben Cooper) $125-150; Oliver Hardy (Halco) $55-65

MADAM BUTTERFLY, ca. 1958. A very rare Wonderland Madam Butterfly rayon costume. This came with a fan. Value $110-125

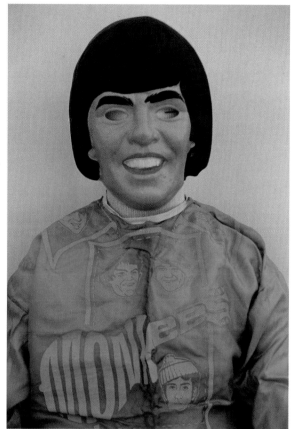

MONKEES; 1960s. Raybert Productions; Bland Charnas. Take the Beatles, emphasize their commercial appeal and make them American, and what do you get? Hey hey—the Monkees! At a time when the Beatles were becoming a bit too adult for the teenyboppers, crooning about tangerine trees and marmalade skies, the tame Monkees simply smiled and acted adorably silly. They appeared on a hit TV show and had several #1 singles, including "Last Train to Clarksville" and "I'm a Believer." The amazing Halloween costumes came in a suit (for the boys) and a mini-dress (for the girls). VALUE FOR EACH: Regular version: $135-$150. Mini-Dress version: $175-250. Value for the set of four: Regular version, $600-$650. Mini-Dress version, $750-1000.

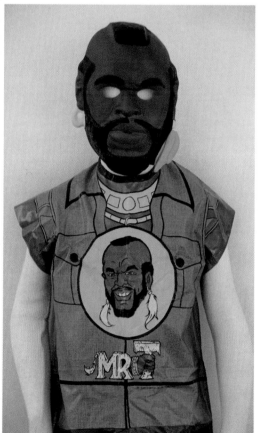

Left:
MR. T; 1983. Ruby-Spears; Collegeville. "I pity the fool!" Mr. T proved to be one of the early 1980s biggest TV stars, mostly due to his stint as B.A. Barracus on *The A-Team*. The mowhawked muscleman made a nifty Halloween costume. Value $20-25.

Right:
MUHAMMAD ALI; 1977. Farmhouse Films; Collegeville. In February of 1964, boxer Muhammad Ali, then known as Cassius Clay, knocked out Sonny Liston and became, quite simply, "the greatest". Perhaps the 20th century's greatest sports hero, Ali starred in the 1977 motion picture, *The Greatest*, playing himself. This Halloween costume, released that same year, was for kids who could dream of being able to "float like a butterfly, sting like a bee!" Great graphics on the suit, although the mask makes Ali look more like Eddie Munster than the greatest boxer of all time. Value $85-95.

THE OSMONDS-DONNY & MARIE, ca. 1977. At the height of Osmondmania with the TV show *Donny and Marie*—came these Halloween outfits. (And yes, they even made one after the youngest Osmond of the bunch, Jimmy.) Aided by appearances on *The Andy Williams Show*, the squeaky-clean Osmonds made a name for themselves with the release of such hits as "One Bad Apple" and "Crazy Horses." But the star of the lot was young Donny, who became a teen idol with such solo offerings as "Go Away Little Girl" and "Puppy Love". Marie also had her share of hits, mainly her remake of "Paper Roses". But when ABC thrust the brother and sister together on *The Donny and Marie Show*—ratings soared. No other program epitomized the schmaltzy polyester era more. And these Halloween costumes—that spotlight the Osmond's perfectly straight, perfectly white teeth—were certainly worn by America's children. It's interesting to note that if you take away the suits and just leave the masks, it's almost impossible to tell them apart! Value for Donny and Marie: $35-45 each. Value for Jimmy: $45-55.

PATRIOTIC, ca. 1968. Ben Cooper. A group of three patriotic rayon costumes.
Miss Liberty, Uncle Sam, and George Washington. Value $65-75 ea

PIRATE, ca. 1953. A cotton Pirate
costume. This is the author, Stuart
Schneider, in his Halloween costume. Value $45-55

ROBIN HOOD, ca. 1959. An un-
marked Robin Hood costume. The
costume probably had a simple face
mask. I have borrowed another
similar vintage Robin Hood mask to
give the costume some personality. It
is all decorated rayon. Value $30-35

ROBIN HOOD, ca. 1959. Ben Cooper Spook
Town. A Robin Hood variation. Value $45-55

SECRET AGENT, ca. 1965. Ben Cooper Spook Town. This is an unlicensed costume, probably inspired by the various secret agent shows that cluttered TV in the middle 1960s. Value $65-70

SIR LANCELOT, ca. 1958. Ben Cooper. A rayon knight's costume with its plastic mask. Value $35-45

TARZAN, ca. 1975. Edgar Rice Burroughs, Inc.; Ben Cooper. Based on the yodeling Edgar Rice Burroughs' jungle character, Tarzan was one of the more popular cultural icons of the century. In the movies, swimmer Johnny Weismuller first brought the jungle denizen to life; on TV, in the 1960s, it was Ron Ely. The ape-man even got his own Saturday morning cartoon, *Tarzan, Lord of the Jungle*. Value $35-40

Far left:
UNCLE SAM, ca. 1930. This boxed Uncle Sam costume may have been made for Halloween, but the design would have been perfect for a 4th of July celebration and parade. It is made of a finished cotton material. Value $125-150

Left:
THE VILLAGE PEOPLE, 1979. Can' t Stop Productions; Super Star. "It's fun to stay at the Y.M.C.A.!" One of the few openly gay-themed Halloween costumes, this biker outfit, based on "Glenn" from the late-1970s pop act the Village People, was for the more adventurous kids. One other Village Person was also turned into a Halloween costume—the Indian. Value $65-70.

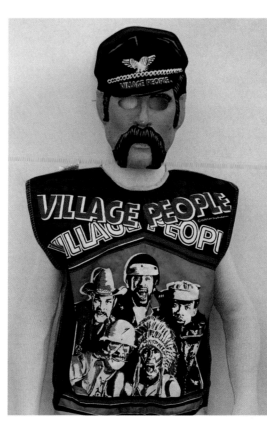

Far left:
W.C. FIELDS, ca. 1972. Ben Cooper. The official name of this costume is "Funny Man." Since W.C.'s name does not appear on the costume or box, this is probably unlicensed. Screened design on vinyl with rayon arms and legs. Value $65-75

Left:
WITCH DOCTOR, ca. 1952. Collegeville. A cotton material with a pull-over cloth mask. Value $45-55

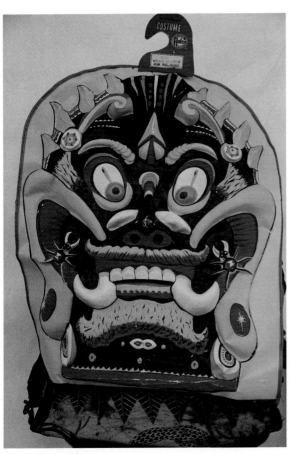

WITCH DOCTOR, 1960s. Halco Masquerade. This is perhaps the most frightening of all Witch Doctor outfits, mainly because the mask is large enough to fit over the entire body of a child. Value $45-55

WRESTLING'S ROAD WARRIORS, ca. 1986. WMMC; Collegeville. A pair of vinyl "Road Warrior" wrestler costumes of "Animal" and "Hawk". Value $45-55 ea.

BOZO THE CLOWN, ca. 1963. Ben Cooper. Any child who grew up between 1950 and 2000 knows who Bozo is— everyone's favorite TV clown. He had two shocks of bright orange hair, and to those with an unnecessary fear of clowns, the sight of his greasepainted facade surely did not help. This Halloween costume— an elegant rayon playsuit—captures him to a tee. Bozo has hair attached to the mask and his name appears on his sleeve cuffs. Value $65-70

BOZO THE CLOWN, ca. 1966. Ben Cooper. A rayon Bozo variation. $40-45

CLOWN, ca. 1956. Collegeville. A rayon Circus Clown costume with a starched cloth mask. Value $45-50

Above right:
CLARABELL THE CLOWN, ca. 1956 Peter Puppet Playthings, Inc. If the children wanted to go trick-or-treating as a clown, what better one than this— Clarabell from *Howdy Doody,* at one time played by Bob Keeshan, future Captain Kangaroo. At *Howdy Doody's* end, in 1960, Clarabell looked forlorn and uttered the only two words he would ever say on-air: "Goodbye, kids." This particular costume would have had a mask, and the shoes (not shown) are simple decorated pieces of cardboard. I am sure that this is the clown that gave me nightmares as a child. I once had the opportunity to meet Clarabell at the opening of a local cleaners, but I would not go near him and told my mother to take me away from there.
Value $125-150

CLOWN, ca. 1920. This homemade clown costume may have been made for Halloween or it may have been made about 1910 for the appearance of Halley's Comet. A sewn cotton material. Value $100-125

CLOWN, ca. 1963. A Clown rayon costume sold at the Grants Stores. Value $25-30

CLOWN, ca. 1963. Ben Cooper. Made of rayon. Value $25-30

CLOWN, ca. 1963. Halco. Compare this rayon outfit to the Ben Cooper produced during the same year. Value $25-30

CLOWN, ca. 1967. Ben Cooper. Made of rayon. Value $25-30

Far left:
CLOWN, ca. 1968. Collegeville. A clown costume of decorated rayon. Value $20-25

Left:
HOBO, ca. 1958. Collegeville Deluxe. Made of cotton. The costume came with a derby hat, bow tie, mask with hair, pants and a jacket. All of it very well made. Value $65-75

Princesses & Fairies

BLUE FAIRY, ca. 1958. Ben Cooper. This "Magic-glo" Blue Fairy costume came with a "glo-in-the-dark" mask. A decorated cardboard wand was also included. The costume had a screened and glittered design on rayon. I believe that the Blue Fairy may be one of the Disney fairies. Value $50-60

HOBO, ca. 1960. Ben Cooper. Is this an example of a costume, mask, and box gone astray? The box says Hobo, the mask is a Hobo but the costume is more clown than Hobo. Value $25-35

BLUE FAIRY, ca. 1968. Ben Cooper. The mask is translucent. Value $45-50

FAIRY PRINCESS, ca. 1959. Ben Cooper. Made of rayon. Value $45-50

FAIRY PRINCESS, ca. 1968. Ben Cooper. Compare this rayon costume to the 1959 Ben Cooper version. Value $35-40

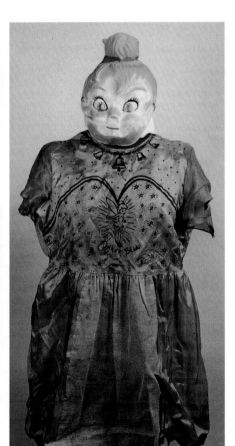

Left:
TINKERBELL, ca. 1957. Walt Disney; Ben Cooper. A rayon Tinkerbell costume with a plastic mask. Value $85-90

Right:
STARLIGHT PRINCESS, ca. 1959. Collegeville. Made of rayon. Value $30-35

ASTEROIDS; 1982. Atari; Collegeville. When it comes to bizarre Halloween costumes, Asteroids should be quite high on the list. What sane child in 1982 actually wanted to go door to door with the mask of a rock over his face? Obviously Collegeville thought enough kids were addicted to the Asteroids arcade game to warrant the creation of this costume. It ranks as one of the all-time goofiest Halloween outfits to hit the stores! Value $45-65

BARBIE, ca. 1975. Mattel; Collegeville. She's the Elvis of Toyland, a pop culture princess that has become the world's most popular doll ever since her debut in 1959. She was beautiful, shapely, and she even got her own (non-threatening) boyfriend, Ken. It's natural that girls wanted to be Barbie, and on Halloween they got their chance. Value $30-35

BARBIE, ca. 1986. Mattel; Ben Cooper. In the 1980s, Barbie had her very own rock band, Barbie and the Rockers. This vinyl costume was inspired by that cool pop act. Value $55-60

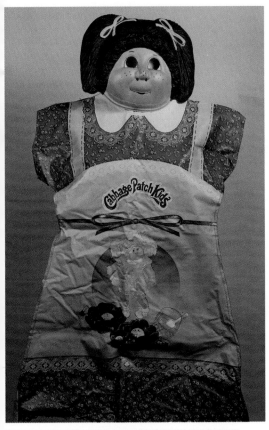 

Far left and left:
CABBAGE PATCH, 1983. O.A.A. Inc.; Ben Cooper. In the early 1980s, a pop culture riot ensued when the limited edition Cabbage Patch Dolls hit toy stores. Every little girl wanted one, and their parents would raise hell, sell the farm, do anything to obtain one. For those kiddies who were thwarted in their attempts to kidnap the Cabbage Patch doll of their dreams, there were these Halloween costumes to appease them. Value $25-30 ea

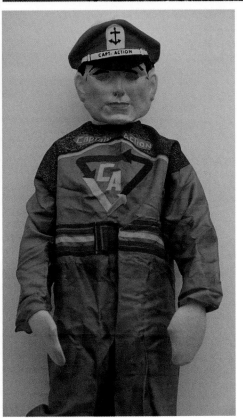

CAPTAIN ACTION, 1966. Ideal Toy Corp.; Ben Cooper. Captain Action was Ideal's answer to Hasbro's massively popular line of fighting men, GI Joe. Unlike Joe's military persona, however, Captain Action could change into any number of classic superheroes and TV favorites—Batman, Aquaman, the Phantom, the Green Hornet, even the Lone Ranger and Tonto. His nemesis was called "Dr. Evil" three decades before Austin Powers' chief villain took that same moniker. The Ben Cooper outfit ranks right up there with Barnabas Collins as one of the all-time rarest to find. It can easily fetch thousands of dollars at toy shows and on eBay.
Value $1800-2500

FARBS, 1973. Mattel; Collegeville. For kids who wanted to go trick-or-treating as their very own redline Hot Wheels car, there's Farbs, the "red Catchup" who was, according to the costume's suit, "the fastastic Car Kook!" An exceptionally rare costume that should be of interest to Hot Wheels collectors as well as Halloween outfit aficionados. Value $100-125.

141

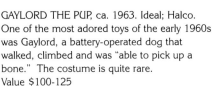

GI JOE, 1960s. Hasbro; Halco. "GI Joe, GI Joe, fighting man from head to toe…on the land, on the sea, in the air…" Five years younger than Barbie, GI Joe was a bulky plasticine he-man introduced as "a poseable action figure for boys" instead of "an icky doll for sissy-girls." Donald Levine of Hasbro came up with the idea, and Joe showed his face in toy stores for the first time in February of 1964—the same month that the Beatles invaded America. The Halloween costume smartly includes Joe's patented facial scar. Value $125-175

GAYLORD THE PUP, ca. 1963. Ideal; Halco. One of the most adored toys of the early 1960s was Gaylord, a battery-operated dog that walked, climbed and was "able to pick up a bone." The costume is quite rare. Value $100-125

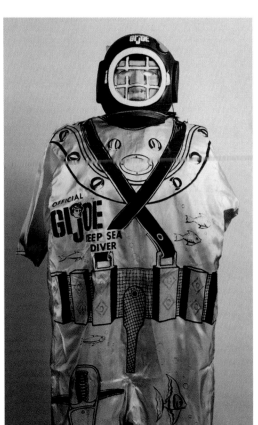

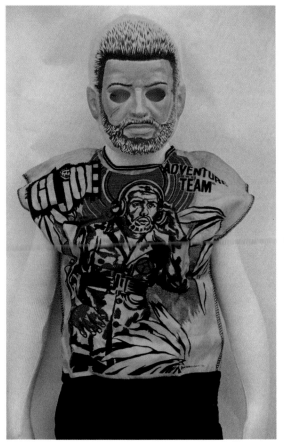

GI JOE, ca. 1969. Hasbro; Halco. A rare rayon "GI Joe Deep Sea Diver" costume. Value $95-115

GI JOE, 1973. Hasbro; Collegeville. In the 1970s, GI Joe changed his hairstyle. He now sported real hair and, in some instances, a beard, as illustrated by this great Halloween costume. Value $45-50

GI JOE, ca. 1986. Hasbro; Ben Cooper. This vinyl GI Joe costume is based on the character "Sgt. Slaughter". Value $25-45

MAJOR MATT MASON, 1967. Mattel; Collegeville. Mattel's answer to GI Joe was the bendable astronaut action figure, Major Matt Mason. Mason and his space-traveling comrades had a friendly alien in the green-faced Calico, but fought against their dangerous alien foe, Scorpio. The Halloween costume is rather rare. Value $150-175

G.I.JOE, ca. 1982. Hasbro; Ben Cooper. GI Joe became miniaturized in the 1980s, no bigger than one of the popular *Star Wars* figurines, but you would never know it by looking at the (full-sized) Halloween costume. Value $25-30

Right:
MICRONAUTS, ca. 1978. Mego; Ben Cooper. Micronauts were popular toys from the late-1970s created by the classic toy company, Mego. This is the vinyl "Biotron" costume. Value $40-45

Far right:
MISSILE COMMAND, 1982. Atari; Collegeville. Another odd outfit based on a video game, Missile Command made an incredibly cool costume. Unlike Asteroids or Q-Bert, kids who wore it didn't feel like they were trick-or-treating as, respectively, a giant rock or an orange anteater-nosed alien; no, kids actually went trick or treating as their very own missile. Value $85-110

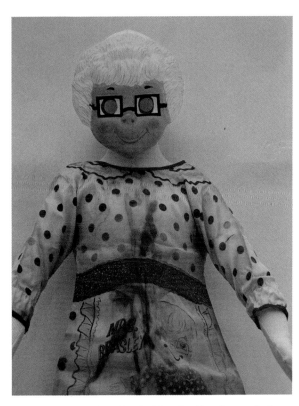

MRS. BEASLEY, 1970. Family Affair Co.; Ben Cooper. Perhaps the most popular TV-based doll of the late 1970s was Mrs. Beasley, Buffy's stuffed pal on the TV series *Family Affair*. The Halloween costume is one of the greats, hard to find and cute as a button. Value $195-225.

MRS. POTATO HEAD, 1950s/1960s. Hasbro; Halco. The best thing about this rare Halloween costume, based on the popular toy, is the illustration on the suit: Mrs. Potato Head flirts with her Potato-headed hubby. Value $125-150

Far left:
PAC-MAN, ca. 1980. Midway Mfg.; Ben Cooper. Of the post-Pong video games, Pac-Man, the yellow ball that keeps running from goblins like Inky and Blinky, remains one of the favorites. This is a very simple mask, barely a step above a smiley face. Value $50-55

Left:
POUND PUPPIES, ca. 1985. Tonka Corp.; Ben Cooper. Pound Puppies were cute toy dogs that were quite popular in the 1980s. Value $20-25

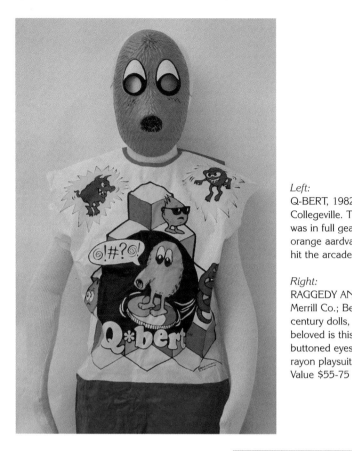

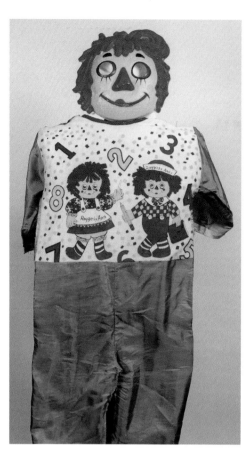

Left:
Q-BERT, 1982. D. Gottlieb Co.;
Collegeville. The video game revolution
was in full gear in 1982 when this
orange aardvark-nosed alien, Q-Bert,
hit the arcades. Value $65-75

Right:
RAGGEDY ANN, ca. 1965. The Bobbs-
Merrill Co.; Ben Cooper. Of all 20th-
century dolls, perhaps the most
beloved is this cute ragamuffin with
buttoned eyes. This costume, an early
rayon playsuit, is quite sweet.
Value $55-75

Below:
RUBICK'S CUBE, ca. 1982. Ideal Toy Company;
Collegeville. This ranks with Asteroids and The
Visible Man among the world's weirdest costumes.
The Rubik's Cube was a plastic toy that challenged
the mind to solve the complicated cubed puzzle.
Value $50-55

Below:
RAGGEDY ANN, ca. 1967. The Bobbs-Merrill
Co.; Ben Cooper. A variation of the classic
Raggedy Ann costume. Value $45-50

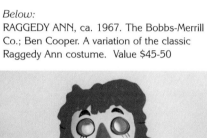

RAGGEDY ANN, ca. 1977. The Bobbs-Merrill Co.;
Ben Cooper. This is a vinyl variation of the Raggedy
Ann outfit. Value $20-25

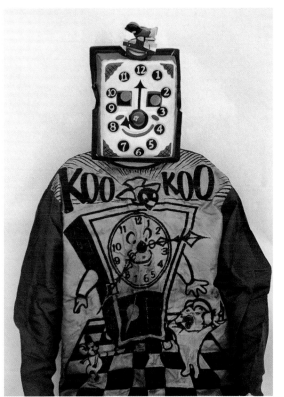

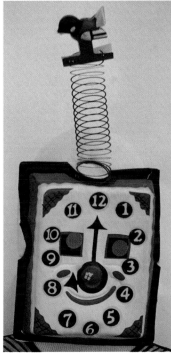

SHOGUN WARRIOR, ca. 1977. Mattel; Ben Cooper. Shogun Warriors were some of the coolest late-1970s toys—giant robots that shot missiles out of their arms. Value $40-45

SLINKY, 1960s. James Industries; Ben Cooper. "It walks the stair without a care and shoots so high in the sky! Bounce up and down, and just like a clown, everyone knows it's Slinky!" The theme song infiltrated itself in the minds of all children. The ever-popular spring-toy made for some mighty odd costumes, especially this one of a Slinky Clock. Value $75-85.

Left:
SLINKY, 1960s. James Industries; Ben Cooper. Another odd costume based on the popular Slinky toy. This is a Slinky Elephant where the elephant's trunk is designed like the spring toy. Value $85-95.

Right:
TEDDY BEAR, ca. 1972. Collegeville. A generic vinyl costume. Value $20-25

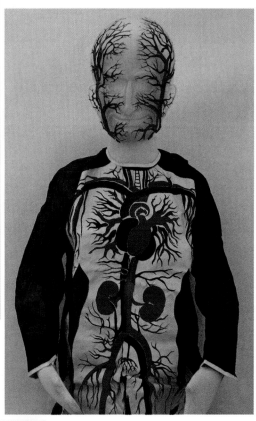

TEDDY RUXPIN, ca. 1985. Worlds of Wonder; Ben Cooper. This vinyl costume was based on the popular Teddy Ruxpin toy—a robotic bear that could talk to its owner. Value $20-25

TROLL, 1960s. Collegeville. This is a tough-to-find Troll rayon costume with "Velvet Touch" decorations. The mask has added hair. Value $65-70

THE VISIBLE MAN; 1960s. Model Kit; Collegeville. If we ranked these Halloween costumes from worst to absolute best, by far the finest—top of the list—should be this costume, modeled after a plastic model, The Visible Man. It's just splendid, from the veiny feet all the way up to freaky transparent mask. What kid was brave enough to want to trick-or-treat as this walking anatomy-lesson? Extremely rare. Value $175-225.

Left and far left:
WRINKLES, ca. 1981. Wrinkles, Inc.; Collegeville. Here is a pair of costumes modeled after the toy dogs known as Wrinkles—one is a boy, the other a girl. Value $20-25 each.

Miscellaneous Costumes

Costumes for Pretty Waitresses

Choosing between these fair young maids is difficult, so we will leave the matter open.

The pumpkin girl's apron is made of orange crepe paper with features cut from black and a bib and tendrils of green crepe paper. Her waiting mate has fashioned an apron of orange crepe paper and trimmed it with cat and kittens nine. These may be found in Decorated Crepe No. H833. The head band trimmed with Pumpkin Seals No. H577 and the cap, which is a large circle of crepe paper gathered to fit the head, are equally easy to make.

Other costumes are shown on pages 25 and 26.

CREPE COSTUMES, ca. 1921. A pair of costumes made with Dennison crepe paper.

CREPE COSTUMES, ca. 1922. A pair of costumes made with Dennison crepe paper.

CREPE COSTUMES, ca. 1923. A group of costumes made with Dennison crepe paper.

CREPE COSTUMES, ca. 1930. A pair of costumes made with Dennison crepe paper.

CREPE COSTUMES, ca. 1925. A pair of costumes made with Dennison crepe paper.

FLASHY THE PUP, ca. 1958. A rayon Flashy The Pup costume missing its mask. Value $50-55

Left:
HAUNTED MANSION MR. SPOOKY, ca. 1970. Walt Disney; Ben Cooper. This Haunted Mansion Mr. Spooky costume is a screened design on a vinyl. Mr. Spooky was one of the three hitchhiking ghosts you'd find at the end of Disneyland's Haunted Mansion ride. The popular attraction first opened in August of 1969 and was designed as a creepy Victorian house filled with spiders and hundreds of ghosts and goblins. The attraction's popularity over the past years has been incredible, and there is a whole collector's segment of people who collect solely Haunted Mansion items. This is certainly one of the top pieces on their want list. Value $250-300

HOOT N'TOOT, ca. 1969. Ben Cooper. The Hoot N'Toot costumes had a kazoo-like tooter in the mouth of the mask. Value $40-45

HOT DOG, ca. 1958. A rare and unusual rayon Hot Dog costume. This may not have had a mask. Value $100-125

HULA GIRL, 1960s. Halco Masquerade. This big-headed mask fits almost around the entire body of a child. Value $45-55

OLD FASHIONED GIRL, ca. 1958. Ben Cooper. An unusual Old Fashioned Girl rayon "Glitter Glo" costume with a starched cloth mask. (This is one of the later uses of a cloth mask.) Value $65-70

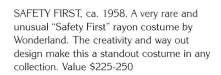

SAFETY FIRST, ca. 1958. A very rare and unusual "Safety First" rayon costume by Wonderland. The creativity and way out design make this a standout costume in any collection. Value $225-250

Costume Accessories

A wonderful costume accessory is the crepe paper Halloween apron. They are rare, made from the 1910s to 1920s, and are mostly crepe paper with a sewn cloth boarder and tie strings. Crepe paper rolls were among the earliest Halloween decorations and one of the most attractive and flexible to use. The designs on the crepe were repeated about every 24 to 30 inches. Crepe was used to decorate walls, tables and even made into costumes. It could be formed into ropes or Spanish moss or ruffles or fringe. The designs were silk screened onto the paper, a very labor intensive process, especially when multiple colors were used, since each color was applied separately.

The major American producer of early paper Halloween supplies was the Dennison Paper Company. They began selling Halloween crepe about 1910. Their output was incredible and the quality and design of their products was excellent. In 1912 Dennison's made four Halloween designs in crepe—"Witch and Kettle", "Witch Parade", "Cats and Bats" and "Yellow Pumpkins". By 1920, they had dozens of designs and some were made into aprons. They are very rare as most were thrown away after one wearing. Other companies such as American Tissue Mills made aprons from their crepe paper stock. Identification is usually made by the design on the apron. The aprons were 18 to 22 inches tall.

One occasionally finds wigs with costumes. It is difficult to determine if these were created as Halloween accessories or as theatrical accessories. Halloween wigs were not high quality items as they were made to be worn once on Halloween, while theatrical pieces were made to be worn many times and needed to be of a higher quality. Few collectors find wigs to be of much interest. Those in their original boxes are collectible, but old costume wigs without boxes do not have much value. Boxed deluxe costumes occasionally came with wigs, with many permanently attached to the mask.

Halloween Aprons

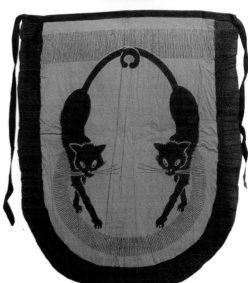

Above left:
CREPE APRON, ca. 1913. Witches in the sky. About 18 inches tall. Value $75-85

Above center:
CREPE APRON, ca. 1915. Dancing witch and cat. About 18 inches tall. Value $75-85

Above right:
CREPE APRON, ca. 1916. Witch and smiling Jack O'lantern. About 22 inches tall. Value $85-95

Right:
CREPE APRON, ca. 1916. Witch on a broom. Probably a Dennison design, about 22 inches tall. Value $85-95

Far right:
CREPE APRON, ca. 1918. Two black cats. About 18 inches tall. Value $85-95

Left:
CREPE APRON, ca. 1916. Owl and bats. Probably a Dennison design, about 22 inches tall. Value $85-95

Right:
CREPE APRON, ca. 1916. Witches flying over spooky town. About 18 inches tall. Value $85-95

CREPE APRON, ca. 1916. Black cats. About 18 inches tall. Value $85-95

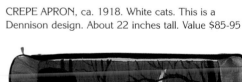

CREPE APRON, ca. 1918. Cats on a Jack O'lantern. A Dennison design about 22 inches tall. Value $85-95

CREPE APRON, ca. 1918. White cats. This is a Dennison design. About 22 inches tall. Value $85-95

Right:
CREPE APRON, ca. 1918. Cloud effect with witches. This is a Dennison design and is about 22 inches tall. Value $85-95

Far right:
CREPE APRON, ca. 1922. Singing and strumming cat. About 22 inches tall. Value $85-95

Trick-or-Treat Bags

Halloween is the time for trick-or-treating. Trick-or-treating began as an attempt to stop vandals from trashing the town on Halloween. Kids used Halloween as a time for playing tricks on neighbors. Shopkeepers began to bribe the children to stop the tricks. In the late 1920s, civic groups in the Northeastern United States began to organize groups of children to call on homes and businesses for treats and pennies. By the 1930s, the custom was established and was spreading across the country. The trick-or-treat sack or bag evolved as a way to carry home the goodies.

The earliest trick-or-treat bags, (called "sacks," west of Ohio) were probably pillow cases or small baskets. The commercially decorated ones, with Halloween pictures, did not appear until the 1940s. Generally, the earliest bags were made of cloth and were about 14 to 20 inches tall, so those could be dated as late 1940s to early 1950s (although some still appear in costume catalogs in the early 1960s). By the 1950s, numerous stores and companies were offering paper sacks with their names or products shown. Parents could also buy decorated orange and black sacks for five or ten cents. In the 1950s, bags were smaller than today's shopping bag (about twelve inches tall) and had a loop handle (another four to six inches). In the photos, you can recognize them as they look like they have a single strap going up from the middle of the bag. It is actually going from side to side. In the late 1950s and early 1960s, the bags were still small shopping bag size (about 14 inches) with a typical shopping bag handle of rolled brown kraft paper attached at two points on each side of the top of the bag. Also made during this time were the semi-rigid plastic bags with the raised image on the outside, and the red or green plastic bags.

In the mid-1960s, as kids began to travel further and stay out longer to get more candy, you begin to see a large shopping-bag style trick-or-treat bag and a few heavy plastic bags appear. Most of these paper sacks with witches, ghosts, bats, and devils upon them were gone by the 1970s. The 1970s were a strange time for bags. The stores began to emphasize their advertising rather than the trick or treat theme and although bags were made, there are very few memorable ones. Some interesting trick-or-treat sacks that were sold in the 1980s are worth collecting. The '90s was almost all thin plastic bags with a few interesting bags coming from McDonald's restaurants along with party stores or stationary stores. Supermarkets seasonally offer plastic shopping sacks with a Halloween design and warnings about safety.

Trick-or-treat sacks are actually very hard to find. Kids dragged them along the ground, tearing out their bottoms, or they were ripped apart by the young trick or treaters, and afterward thrown out. Even though they are tough to find, the majority sell for under $15.

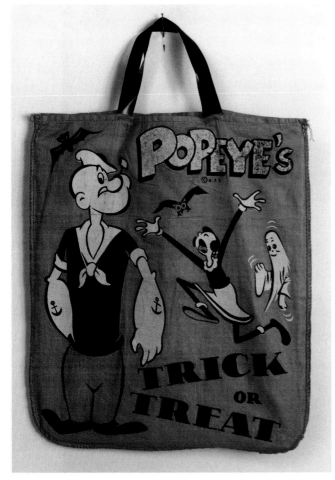

TRICK OR TREAT BAG, ca. 1948. A rare cloth bag showing Popeye and Olive Oyl. The earliest commercially decorated bags are cloth with plastic handles. About 14 inches tall with handle. Value $150-165

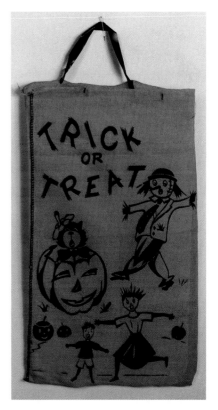

TRICK OR TREAT BAG, ca. 1948. An early cloth bag with a crude design. The earliest commercially decorated bags are cloth with plastic handles. About 20 inches tall with handle. This is the only example of this bag that we have seen to date. Value $150-165

Left and above:
TRICK OR TREAT BAG, ca. 1950. A group of cloth bags with Halloween scenes. The earliest commercially decorated bags are cloth with plastic handles. About 14 inches tall with handle. Value $50-65 ea.

TRICK OR TREAT BAG, ca. 1952. A nice early Walgreen's bag with a 1951 copyright date. About 14 inches tall. Value $35-40

TRICK OR TREAT BAG, ca. 1952. An early paper bag with an advertisement for drinks by Lincoln. About 12 inches tall. Value $55-65

TRICK OR TREAT BAG, ca. 1955. A bag that says it all. "Shell Out". About 12 inches tall with handle. Value $40-45

TRICK OR TREAT BAG, ca. 1955. A simple Halloween scene. About 14 inches tall. Value $20-25

TRICK OR TREAT BAG, ca. 1955. A Kahn's Weiner World bag. About 12 inches tall. Value $20-25

TRICK OR TREAT BAG, ca. 1957. An owl and Jack O'lantern-faced witch. About 14 inches tall. Value $20-25

TRICK OR TREAT BAG, ca. 1957. Orange Crush probably made this bag available when you bought a case of their orange soda. About 12 inches tall. Value $25-30

TRICK OR TREAT BAG, ca. 1958. A black, white and orange haunted house. About 14 inches tall. Value $20-25

Far left and left:
TRICK OR TREAT BAG, ca. 1959. A wonderful design on this bag makes it a centerpiece of a collection. Both sides are shown. About 14 inches tall with handle. Value $60-75

TRICK OR TREAT BAG, ca. 1959. A wonderful four-sided bag showing kids in trick or treating. The Pirate costume was very popular in the mid-1950s to early 1960s. About 14 inches tall. Value $50-55

TRICK OR TREAT BAG, ca. 1959. A nice bag showing kids in costume trick or treating and holding the same bag. The Hobo costume was very popular in the mid-1950s to early 1960s. About 16 inches tall. Value $50-55

TRICK OR TREAT BAG, ca. 1959. This is a great bag. It shows kids in costume trick or treating. The wonderful thing about this bag is that it was made by Ben Cooper and showed an assortment of their Halloween costumes. About 14 inches tall. Value $45-55

TRICK OR TREAT BAG, ca. 1959. A nice Frisch's Big Boy bag. About 14 inches tall. Value $25-35

TRICK OR TREAT BAG, ca. 1959. A brown bag with a kids in costume trick or treating design. About 14 inches tall. Value $35-45

TRICK OR TREAT BAG, ca. 1959. An orange bag with ghosts. About 12 inches tall. Value $35-45

TRICK OR TREAT BAG, ca. 1959. A simple Halloween scene. About 16 inches tall. Value $25-30

TRICK OR TREAT BAG, ca. 1960. The imagery is wonderful on this bag. It shows kids out playing tricks and visiting houses. There is even a kid holding the same bag on the left side of the image by the fence. About 14 inches tall with handle. Value $55-65

TRICK OR TREAT BAG, ca. 1960. There were a few bags made like this. They have a three-dimensional plastic face similar to a Halloween mask. They are very fragile and prone to cracking. About 14 inches tall with handle. Value $60-65

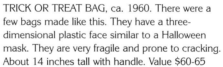

TRICK OR TREAT BAG, ca. 1960. This has a three-dimensional plastic face and a cloth back. It is very fragile and prone to cracking. About 14 inches tall with handle. Value $50-55

TRICK OR TREAT BAG, ca. 1960. A vinyl and cloth bag. About 12 inches tall without its handle. Value $20-25

TRICK OR TREAT BAG, ca. 1962. This bag has great graphics. It shows kids in costume trick or treating. The Jack O'lantern "bag" that the girl is holding indicates that it is later than the 1950s. About 14 inches tall. Value $45-55

TRICK OR TREAT BAG, ca. 1964. I've always enjoyed the bags that leave space for the child's name and address. This says that it lived in a much more gentle time when small kids could go out trick or treating in their neighborhood without their parents. About 14 inches tall. Value $20-25

TRICK OR TREAT BAG, ca. 1964. Lots of Jack O'lanterns. About 16 inches tall. Value $20-25

TRICK OR TREAT BAG, ca. 1964. Witch and cat on a broomstick. About 16 inches tall. Value $20-25

TRICK OR TREAT BAG, ca. 1964. A hobo or gangster who spells gud. About 18 inches tall. Value $20-25

TRICK OR TREAT BAG, ca. 1964. A sweet grouping of Halloween images. About 16 inches tall. Value $20-25

TRICK OR TREAT BAG, ca. 1964. Two kids have stolen a witch's broom and kicked her off. About 21 inches tall. Value $35-40

TRICK OR TREAT BAG, ca. 1964. Esso gasoline gave away bags at their gas stations. Put a tiger in your bag. About 20 inches tall. Value $20-25

TRICK OR TREAT BAG, ca. 1965. Kids in costume approaching a haunted house. About 14 inches tall. Value $35-40

TRICK OR TREAT BAG, ca. 1965. Witch on a broomstick flying over a road. About 14 inches tall. Value $20-25

TRICK OR TREAT BAG, ca. 1967. A nice large
Howdy Beef burgers bag. About 20 inches tall
with handle. Value $20-25

TRICK OR TREAT BAG, ca. 1966. A very rare Green
Hornet plastic trick or treat bag offered by Vernor's soft
drink company. About 14 inches tall. Value $50-65

TRICK OR TREAT BAG, ca. 1967. This is a
vinyl bag. The artwork has kind of a Rockey
and Bullwinkle cartoon quality. About 16
inches tall. Value $35-45

TRICK OR TREAT BAG, ca. 1975. A Scott's Store
advertising bag that I feel looks older than it is.
About 16 inches tall. Value $20-25

Halloween Hats

Party hats are probably one of the most reasonably priced Halloween items that you can collect. They rarely sell for more than $25.00 and most are priced at $5 to $10. The "good, better, and best" of hats start with simple orange and black hats of paper, perhaps with a simple design. The simpler designs were typically made in the 1940s and '50s. The better hats have a certain style, such as Art Deco, or have more excit-

ing graphics, added pieces, or perhaps some honeycomb tissue parts. These were more often made in the 1930s. The best hats have multicolored graphics or an added composition attachment; most of these were made in Germany and exhibit high quality lithography. These usually date to the teens or 1920s.

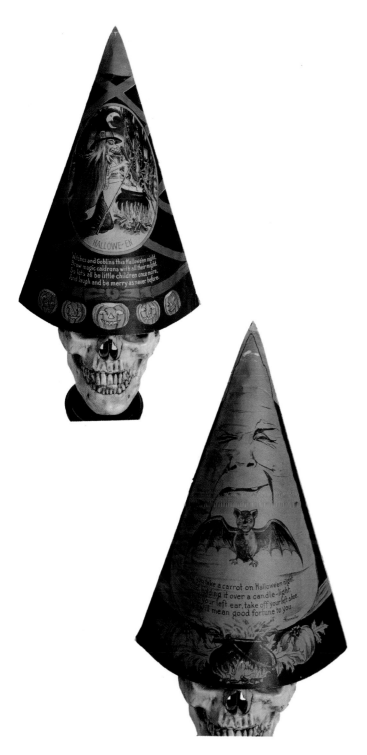

HAT, ca. 1918. A sewn crepe hat with a rat on a pumpkin and a cat face at the top. Value $20-25

HAT, ca. 1915. A beautiful lithographed paper hat made in Germany. Value $85-100

HAT, ca. 1920. A crepe hat. Value $6-9

HAT, ca. 1920. A pumpkin crepe hat, 14 inches tall. Value $25-30

HATS, ca. 1921. Dennison's crepe paper hats and masks.

HAT, ca. 1920. A nice German-made hat. Value $20-25

HATS, ca. 1922. Dennison's crepe paper hats and masks.

HAT, ca. 1925. A sewn crepe hat by Dennison. Value $20-25

HAT, ca. 1927. Dennison's paper hats. Value $12-15 ea.

HAT, ca. 1925. A German-made paper hat. Value $20-25

HAT, ca. 1930. A crepe hat, probably a Dennison design. Value $6-9

HAT, ca. 1930. A sewn crepe hat in an Art Deco Style made by Dennison. Value $20-25

HAT, ca. 1930. A hard to find Japanese-made hat. Value $20-25

HAT, ca. 1930. A hard-to-find Japanese-made hat. Value $12-15

HAT, ca. 1940. A cardboard hat with a witch and cats. Value $10-15

HAT, ca. 1953. A cardboard hat of a ghost escaping the flames. Value $10-15

HAT, ca. 1955. Two crepe and paper hats. Value $10-15 ea.

Masks, Wigs and Fans

Masks that can be found include latex full-head covering pieces, plastic vacuformed faces, paper, and the earlier starched-cloth face coverings. We have stayed away from including examples of full-head covering masks since that deserves a book of its own. All of the costume companies made and sold masks without the costume. There are hundreds of vacuformed masks available to the collector. We have chosen to show masks that came with costumes.

Mask repair: Many of the vacuformed masks have cracks. If the cracks bother you, some can be fixed with plastic model cement. Others take a more specialized glue, like Tenex, while others can only be repaired with slow-curing epoxy. Should you decide to attempt to close up a crack, here is the method that has generally worked for us. Start on a small edge crack that is in an area of the mask that is black. If the glue affects the paint, you can easily retouch most masks with flat black model paint. Use cellophane tape to close the crack on the front side of the mask. Apply glue along the crack inside the mask and let it dry completely (overnight is adequate). When dry, peel off the tape and see if the glue has permanently adhered to the mask. Sometimes it won't work and will peel right off. This calls for a different type of glue. Warning: Too much glue can cause a bulge on the outside of the mask or loss of paint caused by the solvent in the glue affecting the mask.

FAN, ca. 1918. A beautiful stenciled cat fan with cut out eyes. Value $110-125

FAN, ca. 1918. A printed paper and wood fan with cats eating and drinking at a table. Value $110-115

FAN, ca. 1920. Fighting cats on a fence fan. Value $85-100

MASK, ca. 1925. Dennison's paper masks. Value $12-15 ea.

MASK, ca. 1925. A paper black cat mask. Value $12-15

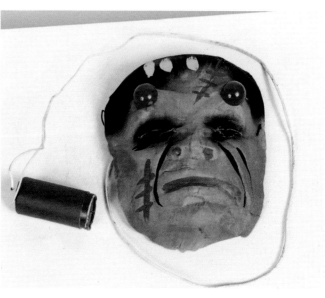

MASK, ca. 1952. A nice early Frankenstein mask with a battery so that the lights at the top of the face could light up. This was probably part of a costume. Value $85-100

WIG, ca. 1938. A box showing the wigs available for Halloween and theatrical use. Value $55-60

WIG, ca. 1954. A box showing the wigs available for Halloween and theatrical use. Value $40-45

Costume Boxes

Left:
BOX, ca. 1930. An Uncle Sam costume. No other maker information.

Right:
BOX, ca. 1934. A great Art Deco "Mask O Ween" box that held the Jail Bird costume. No other maker information.

BOX, ca. 1940. Masquerade Costume box that held a witch's costume with a cape, hat and skirt. No other maker information.

BEN COOPER, ca. 1950. A Devil costume box. Similar boxes can be found without the window.

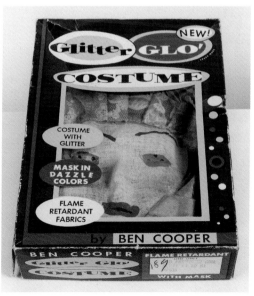

Right:
BEN COOPER, ca. 1952. A wonderful Space Rocket Commando Spotlite box.

Far right:
BEN COOPER, ca. 1958. A Glitter Glo' box.

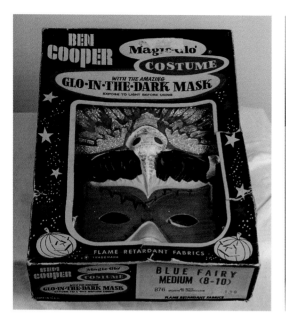

Far left:
BEN COOPER, ca. 1958. A Magic-glo costume with a "glo-in-the-dark" mask.

Left:
BEN COOPER, ca. 1959. A Spook Town box.

Right:
BEN COOPER, ca. 1959. A Famous Name box.

Far right:
BEN COOPER, ca. 1962. A Flick & Trick Lite-Up Mask costume box.

Left:
BEN COOPER, ca. 1963. A T.V. Star box.

Right:
BEN COOPER, ca. 1963. A Masquerade Costume box.

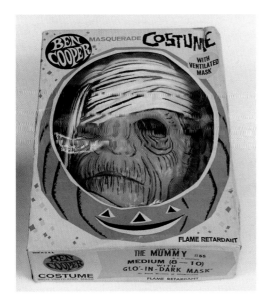

BEN COOPER, ca. 1965. A glow in the dark mask box.

BEN COOPER, ca. 1965. A Color Brite box.

BEN COOPER, ca. 1965. A Magic Glo' box.

BEN COOPER, ca. 1967. A Glitter Glo' Costume box.

BEN COOPER, ca. 1967. A Moving Mouth Mask box.

BEN COOPER, ca. 1967. A Spook Town box.

BEN COOPER, ca. 1968. A TV Hero costume box.

BEN COOPER, ca. 1968. A Nite-Owl Bright costume box.

Right:
BEN COOPER, ca. 1969. A Deluxe Quality costume and mask box.

Far right:
BEN COOPER, ca. 1969. A Hoot N'Toot costume box.

Far left:
BEN COOPER, ca. 1973. A Planet of The Apes box.

Left:
BEN COOPER, ca. 1976. A Rescue Team costume box.

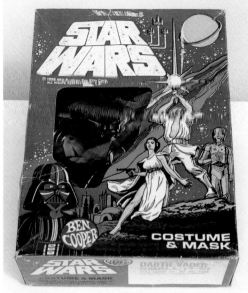

Right:
BEN COOPER, ca. 1977. A Super
Hero costume box.

Far Right:
BEN COOPER, ca. 1977. A Star Wars
costume box

Far left:
BEN COOPER, ca. 1978. A
Science Fiction costume box.

Left:
BEN COOPER, ca. 1982. A
Famous Faces costume box.

Right:
DISNEY BEN COOPER, ca. 1957.
A Walt Disney costume box.

Far right:
DISNEY BEN COOPER, ca. 1958.
A Walt Disney character costume
box.

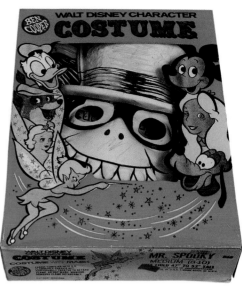

Right:
DISNEY BEN COOPER, ca. 1959. A Walt Disney character costume box.

Far right:
DISNEY BEN COOPER, ca. 1970. A Walt Disney character costume box.

Far left:
WONDERLAND, ca. 1958. A Wonderland costume box.

Left:
BLAND CHARNAS, ca. 1960. A Glow in the Dark Mask costume box.

Right:
BLAND CHARNAS, ca. 1965. A Monkees costume box.

Far right:
GRANTS, ca. 1963. A ventilated mask costume box.

HALCO, ca. 1956. A Masquerade costume box.

HALCO, ca. 1962. A Masquerade costume box.

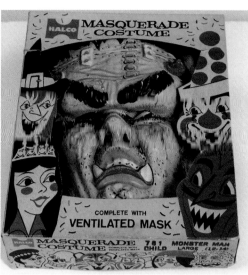

HALCO, ca. 1964. A Masquerade costume box.

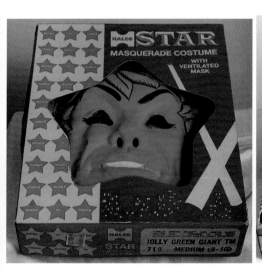

HALCO, ca. 1964. A Masquerade costume box.

HALCO, ca. 1966. A Man From U.N.C.L.E. costume box.

COLLEGEVILLE, ca. 1949. A Masquerade costume box.

COLLEGEVILLE, ca. 1952. A Halloween costume box.

COLLEGEVILLE, ca. 1953. A Halloween Parties Masquerade costume box.

COLLEGEVILLE, ca. 1957. A Bright For Night costume box.

COLLEGEVILLE, ca. 1957. A Famous TV and Comic Book Characters costume box.

COLLEGEVILLE, ca. 1959. A Sparkle Velvet costume box.

COLLEGEVILLE, ca. 1960. A Flame Retarded costume box.

COLLEGEVILLE, ca. 1968. A Halloween Flame Retarded costume box.

COLLEGEVILLE, ca. 1969. A White For Night costume box.

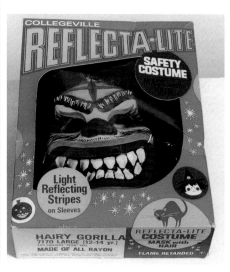

COLLEGEVILLE, ca. 1969. A Reflecta-Lite costume box.

COLLEGEVILLE, ca. 1970. A Safari costume box.

COLLEGEVILLE, ca. 1978. A TV-Comics costume box.

COLLEGEVILLE, ca. 1981. A Wrinkles costume box.

COLLEGEVILLE, ca. 1982. A Looney Tunes costume box.

COLLEGEVILLE, ca. 1982. A Rubik's Cube costume box.

COLLEGEVILLE, ca. 1985. A Scratch'N'Sniff costume box.

Index